High Voice

Disney Songs for Singers

45 Classics

D1591885

ISBN 0-634-08152-7

Wonderland Music Company, Inc.
Walt Disney Music Company

DISTRIBUTED BY

7777 W. BLUEMOUND RD. P.O. BOX 13819 MILWAUKEE, WI 53213

Visit Hal Leonard Online at
www.halleonard.com

Contents

THE BARE NECESSITIES

from Walt Disney's *The Jungle Book*

Words and Music by
Terry Gilkyson

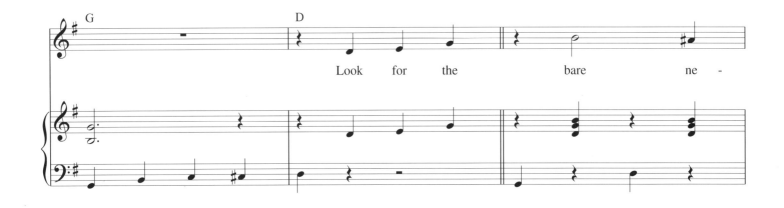

Look for the bare ne-

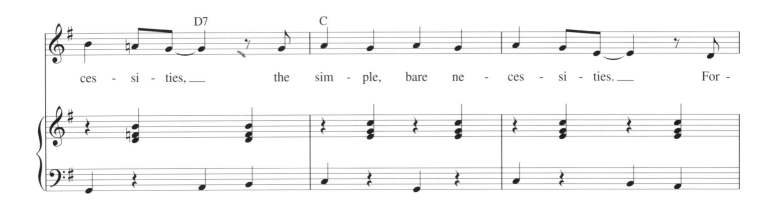

ces - si - ties, __ the sim - ple, bare ne - ces - si - ties. __ For -

get a - bout __ your wor - ries and your strife. I mean the

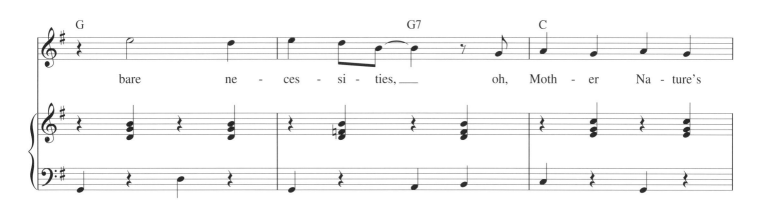

bare ne - ces - si - ties, __ oh, Moth - er Na - ture's

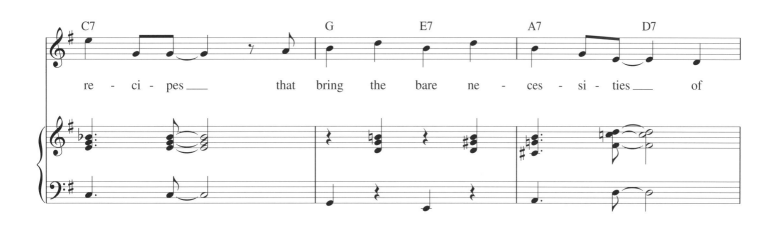

re - ci - pes __ that bring the bare ne - ces - si - ties __ of

life.   Wher - ev - er I wan - der, __
When you pick __ a paw - paw __

wher - ev - er I roam,   I could - n't be
or a prick - ly pear   and you __ pick a

To Coda

fond - er _____ of my big home.
raw paw, ___ well, next time, be - ware.

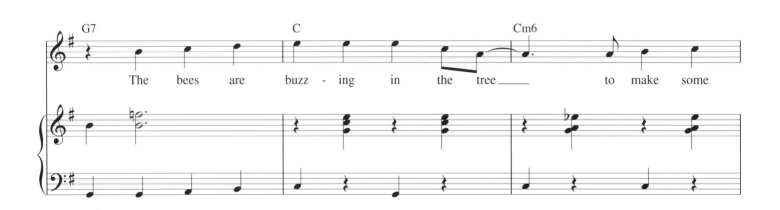

The bees are buzz - ing in the tree _____ to make some

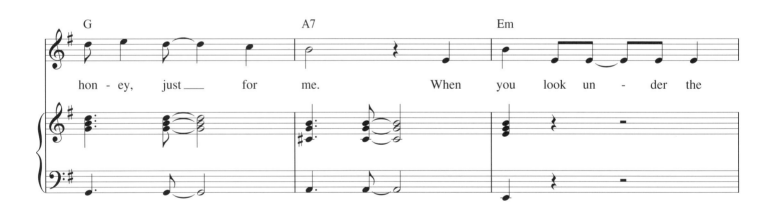

hon - ey, just ___ for me. When you look un - der the

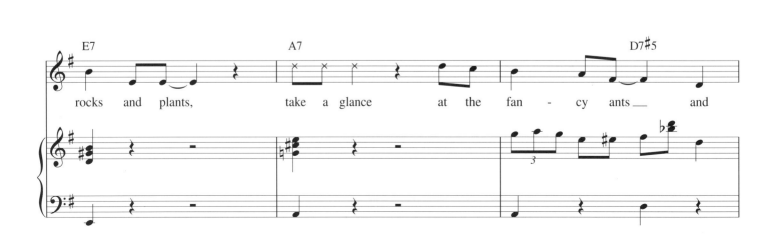

rocks and plants, take a glance at the fan - cy ants ___ and

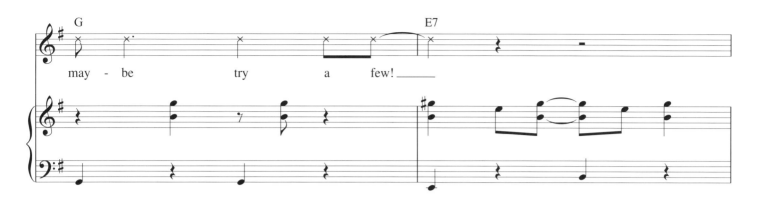

may - be   try   a   few! _____

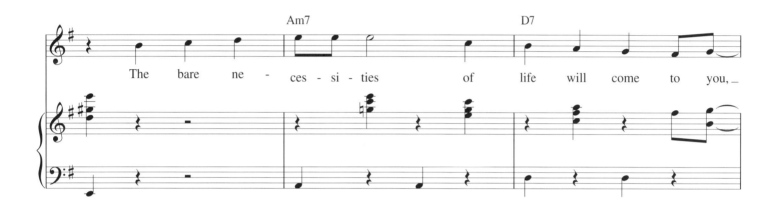

The bare ne - ces - si - ties   of life will come to you, _

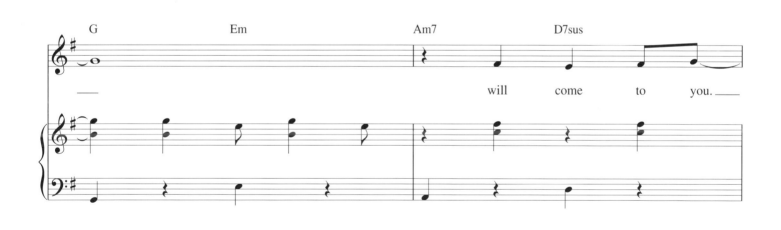

_____   will   come   to   you. ____

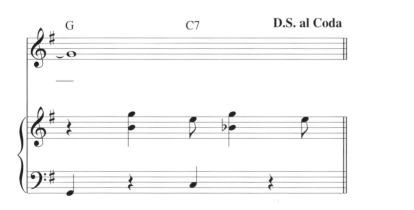

D.S. al Coda

_____

CODA

Don't pick the

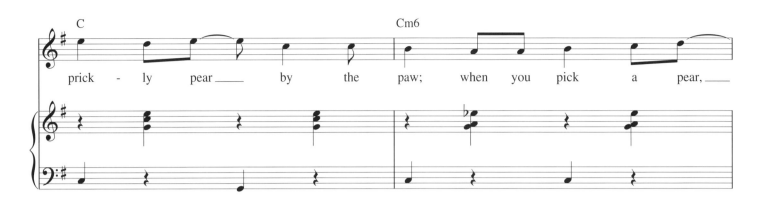

prick - ly pear ___ by the paw; when you pick a pear, ___

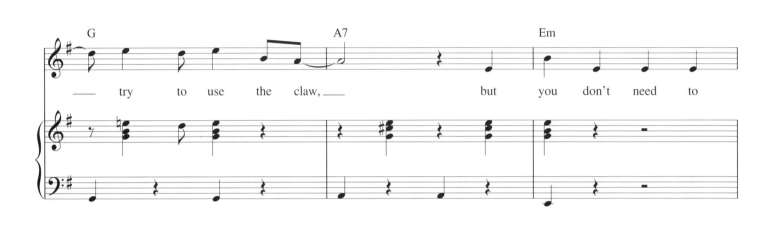

___ try to use the claw, ___ but you don't need to

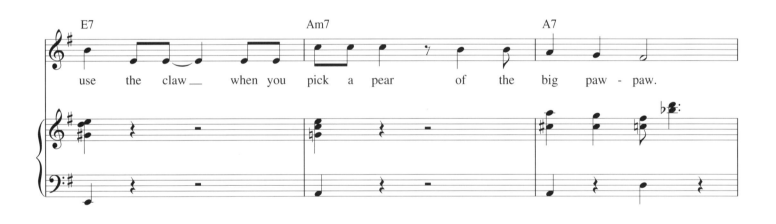

use the claw ___ when you pick a pear of the big paw-paw.

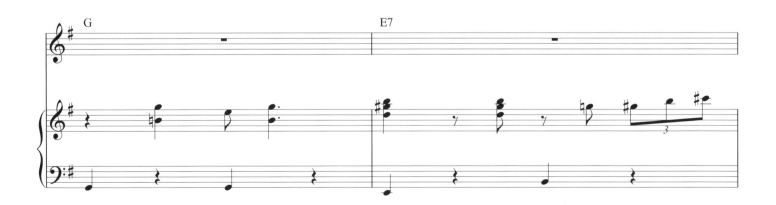

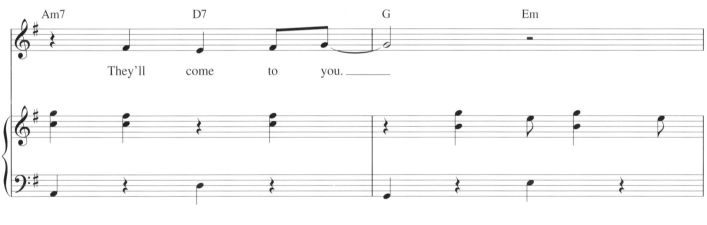

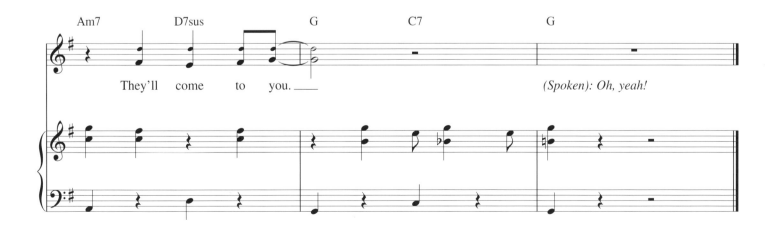

BEAUTY AND THE BEAST

from Walt Disney's *Beauty and the Beast*

Lyrics by Howard Ashman
Music by Alan Menken

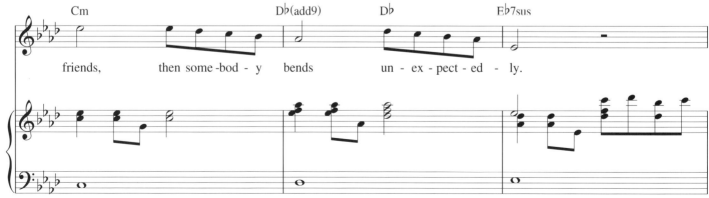

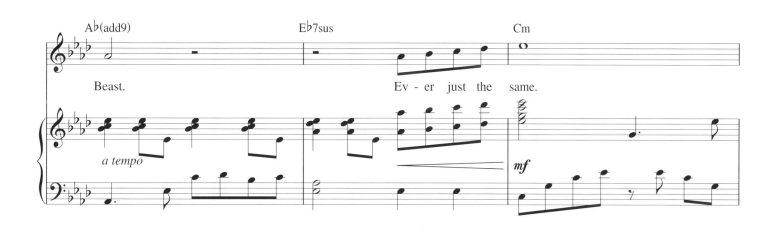

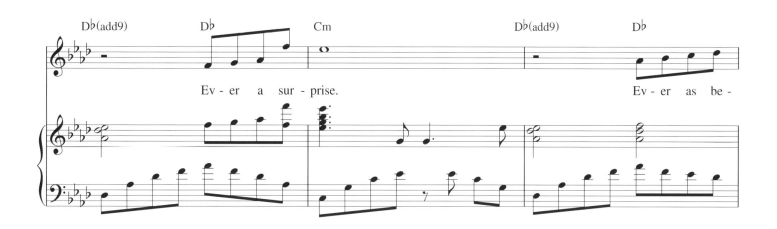

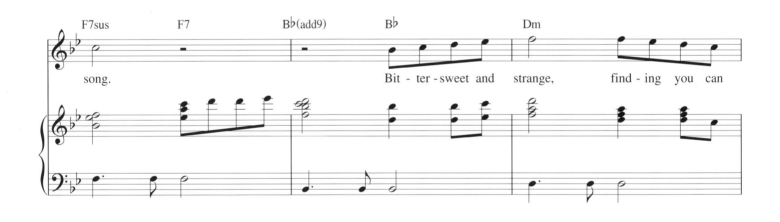

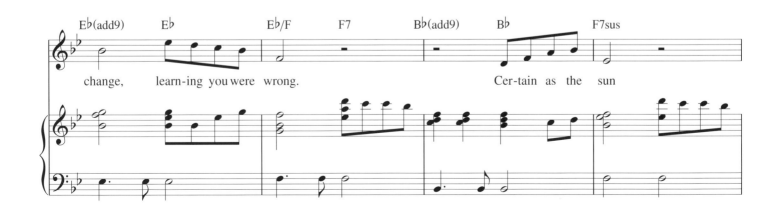

BELLA NOTTE
(This is the Night)
from Walt Disney's *Lady and the Tramp*

Words and Music by Peggy Lee
and Sonny Burke

BIBBIDI-BOBBIDI-BOO
(The Magic Song)
from Walt Disney's *Cinderella*

Words by Jerry Livingston
Music by Mack David and Al Hoffman

CAN YOU FEEL THE LOVE TONIGHT

from Walt Disney Pictures' *The Lion King*

Music by Elton John
Lyrics by Tim Rice

20

CANDLE ON THE WATER
from Walt Disney's *Pete's Dragon*

Words and Music by Al Kasha
and Joel Hirschhorn

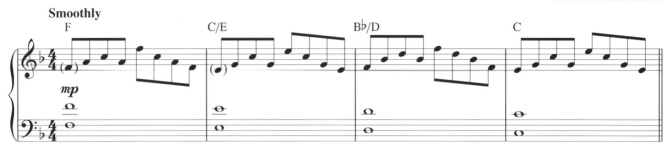

I'll be your can-dle on the wa-ter, my love for you will al-ways
I'll be your can-dle on the wa-ter 'til ev-'ry wave is warm and

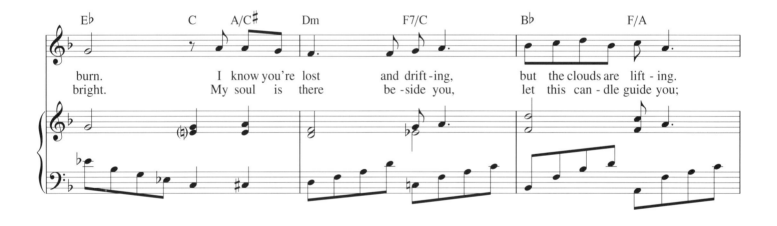

burn. I know you're lost and drift-ing, but the clouds are lift-ing.
bright. My soul is there be-side you, let this can-dle guide you;

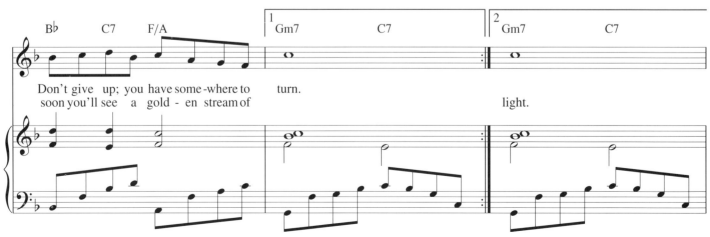

Don't give up; you have some-where to turn.
soon you'll see a gold-en stream of light.

COLORS OF THE WIND

from Walt Disney's *Pocahontas*

Music by Alan Menken
Lyrics by Stephen Schwartz

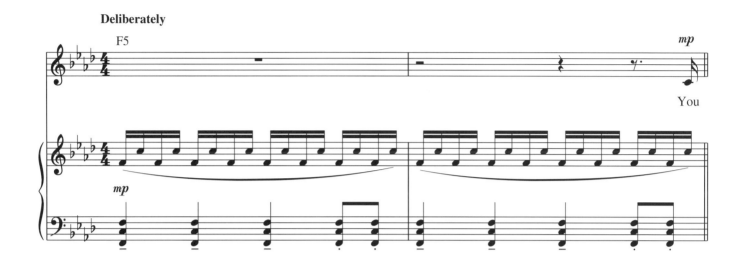

think I'm an ig-no-rant sav-age, and you've been so man-y plac-es, I guess it must be so. But

still I can-not see, if the sav-age one is me, how can there be so much that you don't

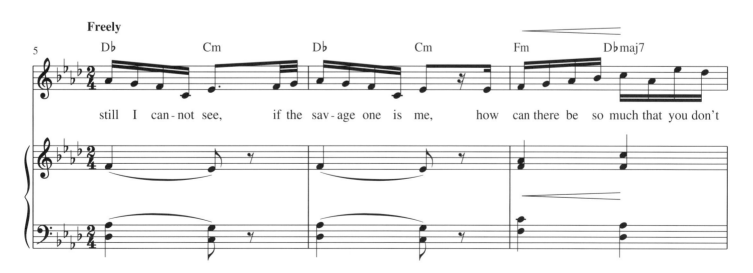

26

CHIM CHIM CHER-EE
from Walt Disney's *Mary Poppins*

Words and Music by Richard M. Sherman
and Robert B. Sherman

Lightly, with gusto

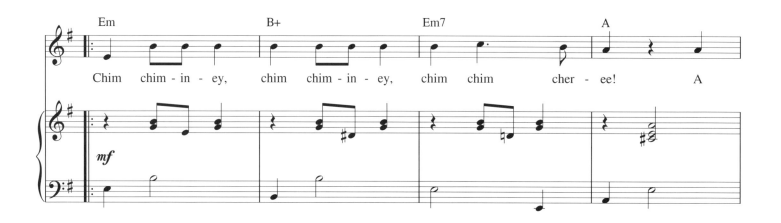

Chim chim-in-ey, chim chim-in-ey, chim chim cher-ee! A

sweep is as luck-y, as luck-y can be.

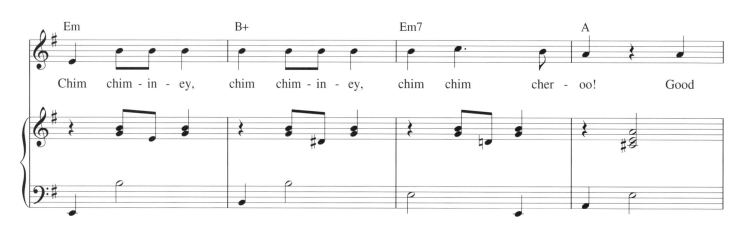

Chim chim-in-ey, chim chim-in-ey, chim chim cher-oo! Good

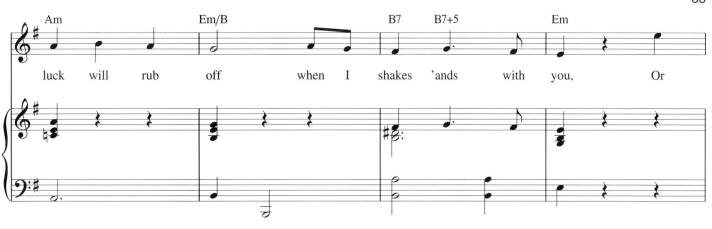

luck will rub off when I shakes 'ands with you, Or

blow me a kiss and that's luck-y, too.

Now, as the the
I choose me

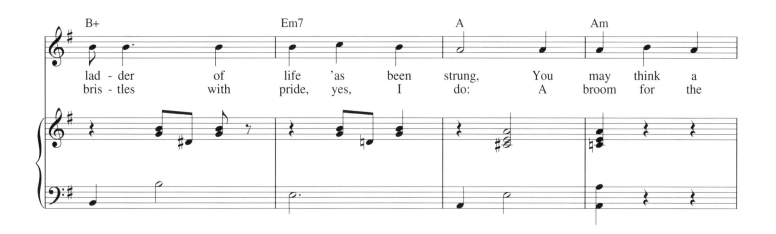

lad-der of life 'as been strung, You may think a
bris-tles with pride, yes, I do: A broom for the

sweep's on the bot - tom - most rung. Though I spends me
shaft and a brush for most the flue. Though I'm cov - ered me with

may in the ash - es and smoke, In this 'ole wide
soot from me 'ead to and me toes, A sweep knows 'e's

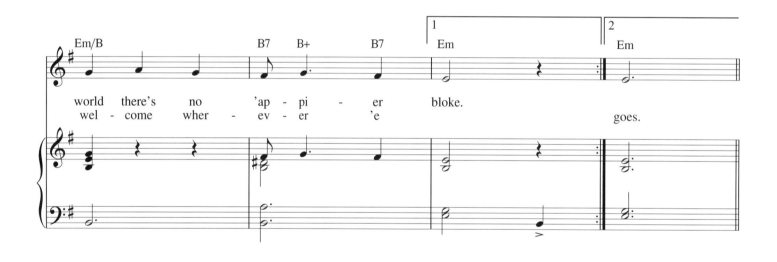

world there's no 'ap - pi - er bloke.
wel - come wher - ev - er 'e goes.

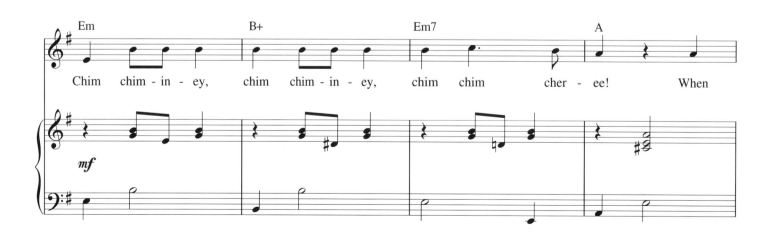

Chim chim - in - ey, chim chim - in - ey, chim chim cher - ee! When

A DREAM IS A WISH YOUR HEART MAKES

from Walt Disney's *Cinderella*

Words and Music by Mack David,
Al Hoffman and Jerry Livingston

When I was a lit- tle { girl, / boy, } my fa- ther used to

say, if trou-ble ev- er trou-bles you, just dream your cares a-

way. A dream is a wish your heart makes ____

FEED THE BIRDS
from Walt Disney's *Mary Poppins*

Words and Music by Richard M. Sherman
and Robert B. Sherman

Slowly, with feeling

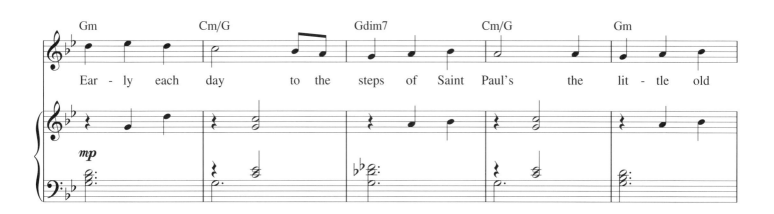

Ear-ly each day to the steps of Saint Paul's the lit-tle old

bird wom-an comes. _____ In her own spe-cial

way to the peo-ple she calls, "Come, buy my

bags full of crumbs. _____ Come feed the lit - tle birds, show them you care, and you'll be glad if you do. _____ Their young ones are

hun - gry, their nests are so bare; all it takes is tup-pence from

42

GIVE A LITTLE WHISTLE

from Walt Disney's *Pinocchio*

Words by Ned Washington
Music by Leigh Harline

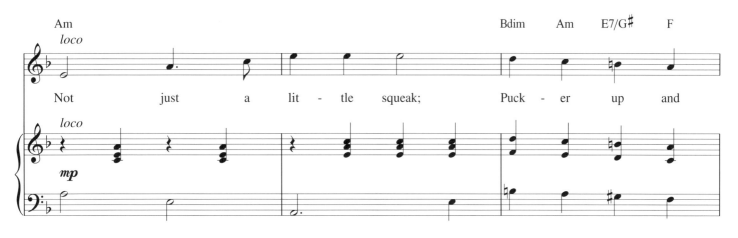

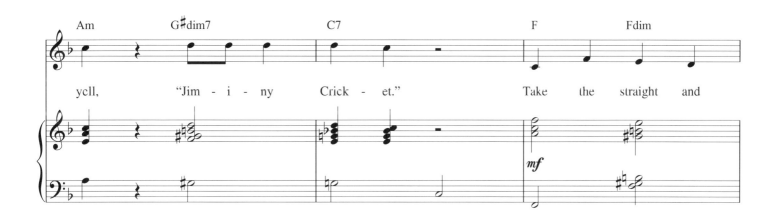

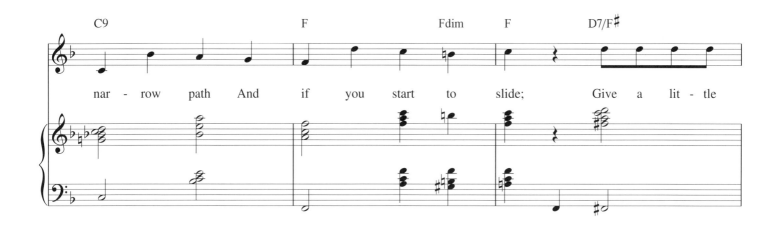

HI-DIDDLE-DEE-DEE
(An Actor's Life For Me)
from Walt Disney's *Pinocchio*

Words by Ned Washington
Music by Leigh Harline

Brightly

The

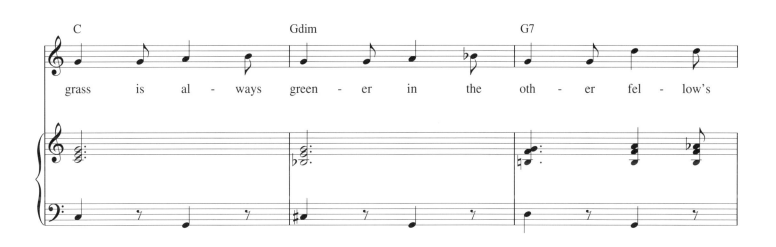

grass is al - ways green - er in the oth - er fel - low's

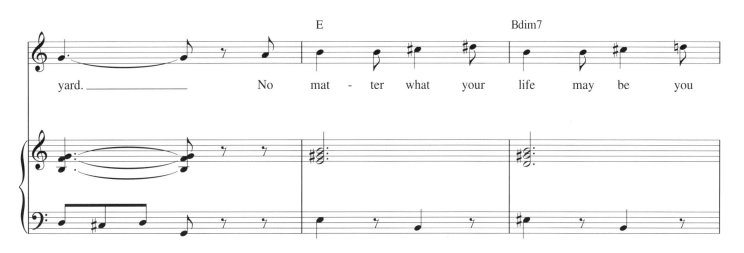

yard. _____ No mat - ter what your life may be you

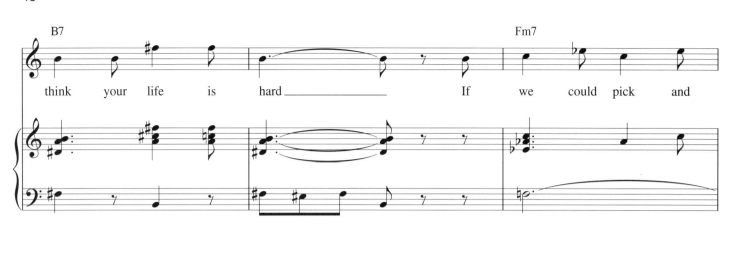

think your life is hard _____ If we could pick and

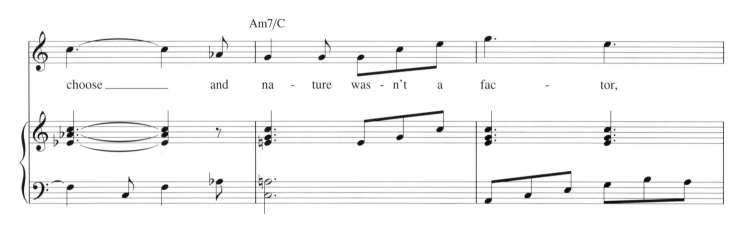

choose _____ and na - ture was-n't a fac - tor,

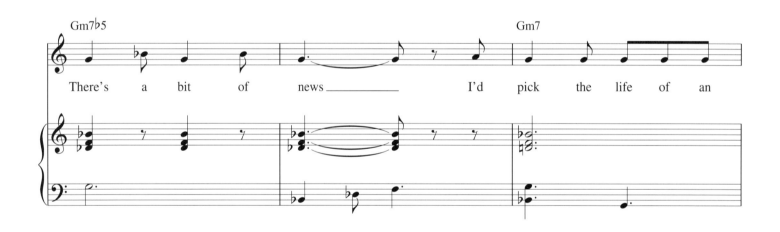

There's a bit of news _____ I'd pick the life of an

act - or.

Hi - did - dle - dee - dee _____ An
Hi - did - dle - dee - dee _____ You

GO THE DISTANCE
from Walt Disney Pictures' *Hercules*

Music by Alan Menken
Lyrics by David Zippel

Moderate Ballad

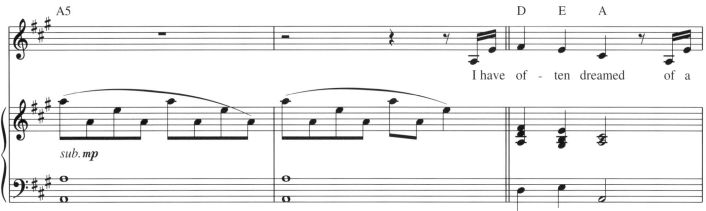

I have of - ten dreamed of a

GOD HELP THE OUTCASTS

from Walt Disney's *The Hunchback of Notre Dame*

Music by Alan Menken
Lyrics by Stephen Schwartz

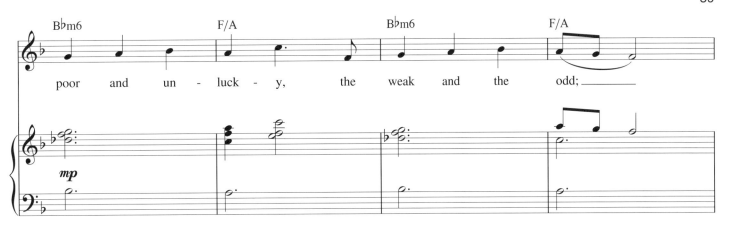

poor and un - luck - y, the weak and the odd; ____

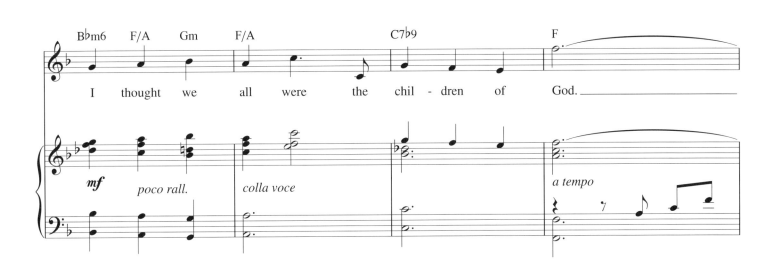

I thought we all were the chil - dren of God. _____

HOME

from Walt Disney's *Beauty and the Beast: The Broadway Musical*

Music by Alan Menken
Lyrics by Tim Rice

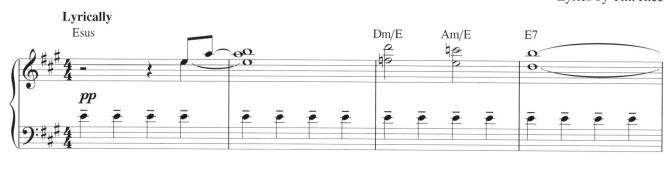

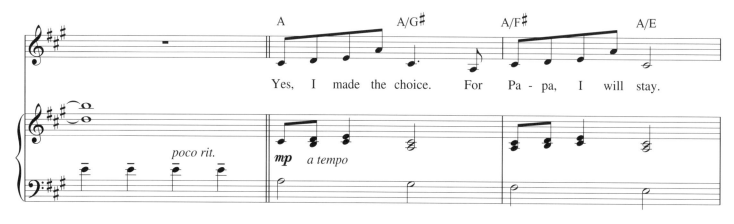

Yes, I made the choice. For Pa-pa, I will stay.

But I don't de-serve to lose my free-dom in this way, you mon - ster! ____

If you think that what you've done ____ is right, well

I BRING YOU A SONG

from Walt Disney's *Bambi*

Words by Larry Morey
Music by Frank Churchill

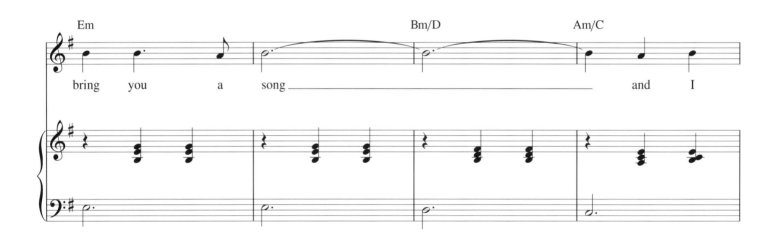

bring you a song _____ and I

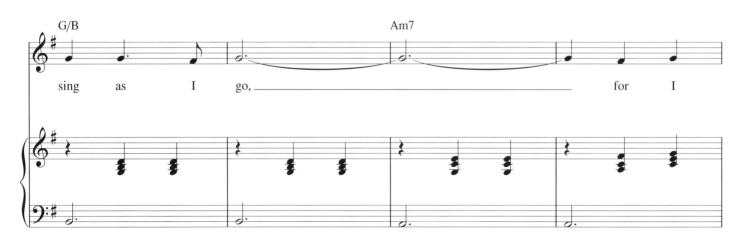

sing as I go, _____ for I

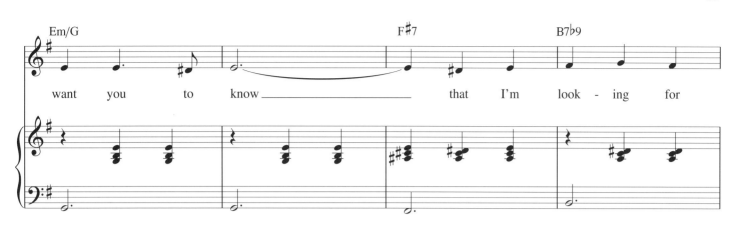

want you to know _____ that I'm look - ing for

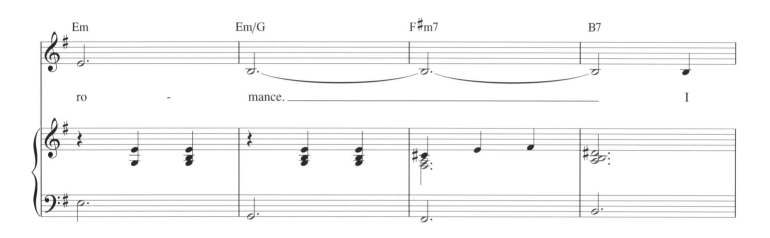

ro - mance. _____ I

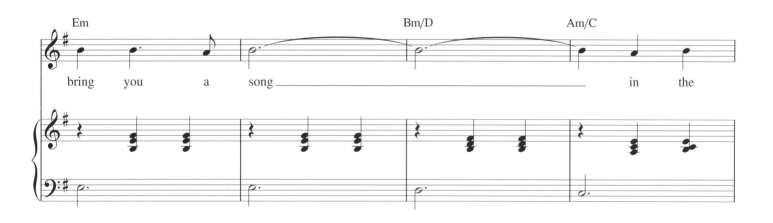

bring you a song _____ in the

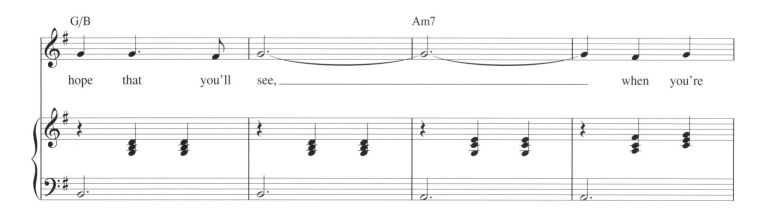

hope that you'll see, _____ when you're

look - ing at me, _____ that I'm look - ing for

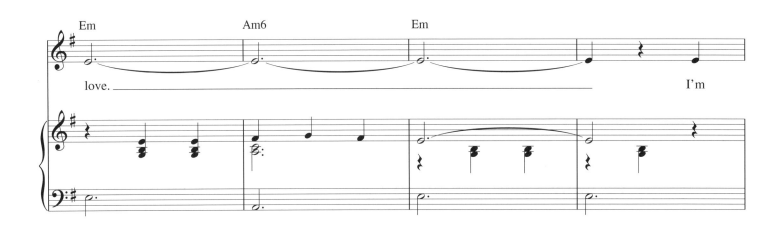

love. _____ I'm

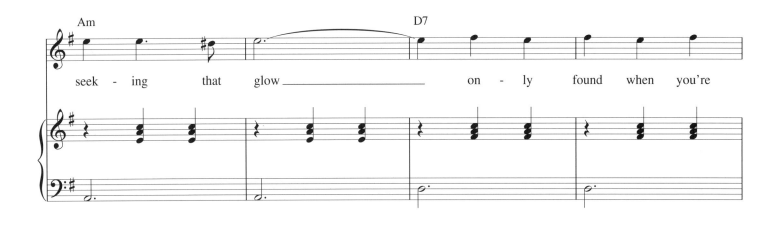

seek - ing that glow _____ on - ly found when you're

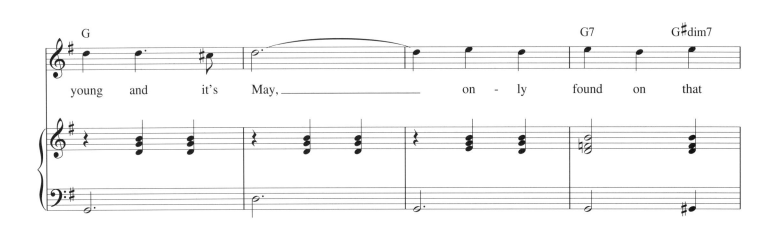

young and it's May, _____ on - ly found on that

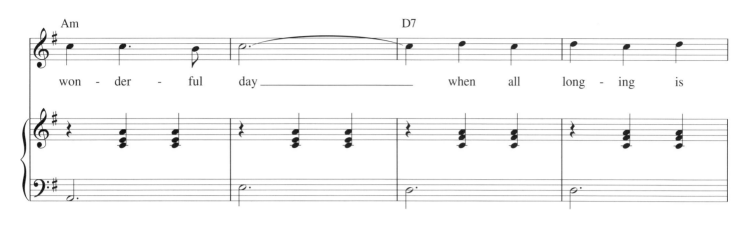

won - der - ful day _____ when all long - ing is

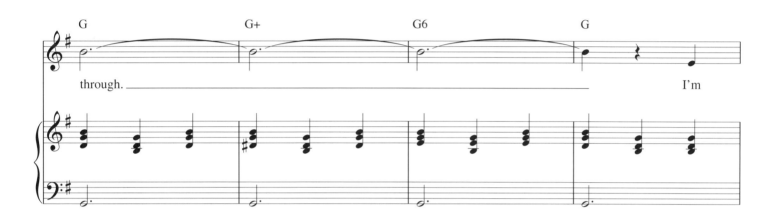

through. _____ I'm

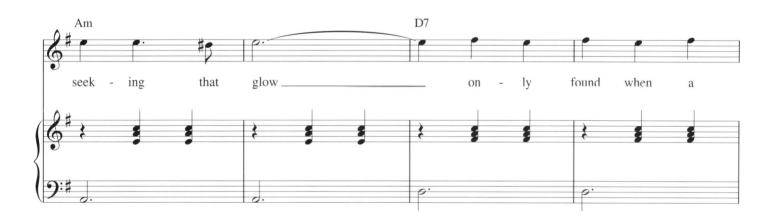

seek - ing that glow _____ on - ly found when a

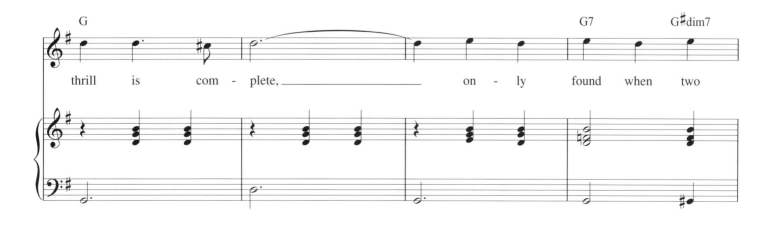

thrill is com - plete, _____ on - ly found when two

I WONDER
from Walt Disney's *Sleeping Beauty*

Words by Winston Hibler and Ted Sears
Music by George Bruns
Adapted from a Theme by Tchaikovsky

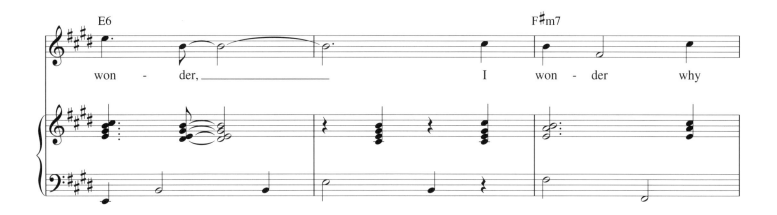

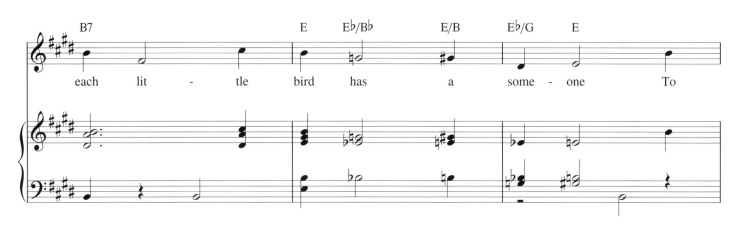

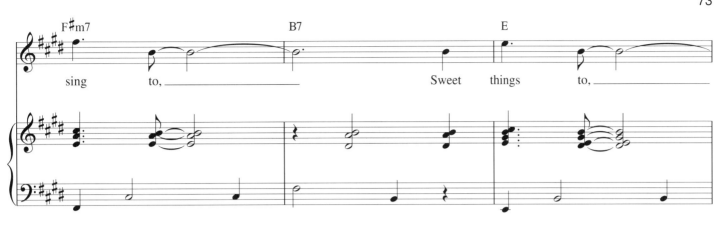

sing   to,_____   Sweet   things   to,_____

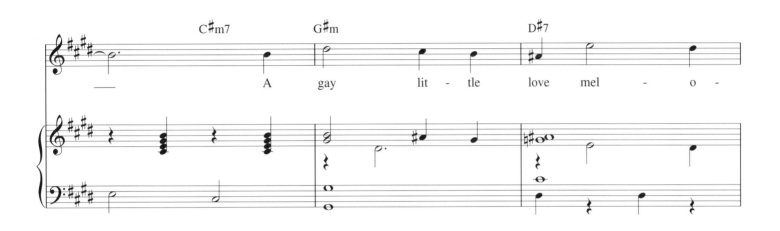

_____   A   gay   lit - tle   love   mel - o -

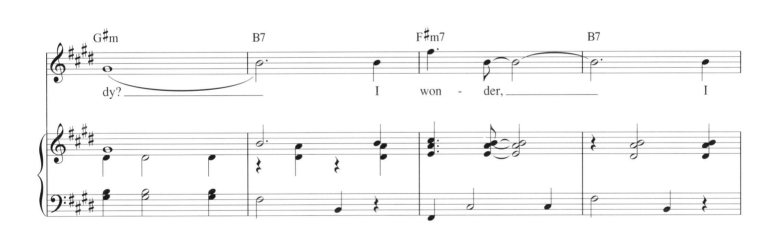

dy?_____   I   won - der,_____   I

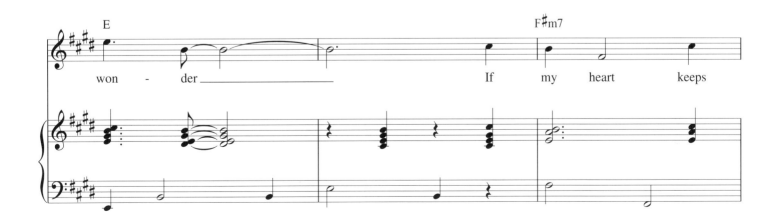

won - der _____   If   my   heart   keeps

sing - ing, will my song go wing - ing To

some - one _____ Who'll find me _____

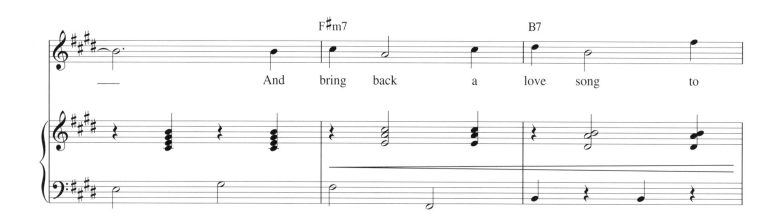

_____ And bring back a love song to

me? I me? _____

I'VE GOT NO STRINGS
from Walt Disney's *Pinocchio*

Words by Ned Washington
Music by Leigh Harline

Hi o the mer - ri - o, I'm as hap - py as can

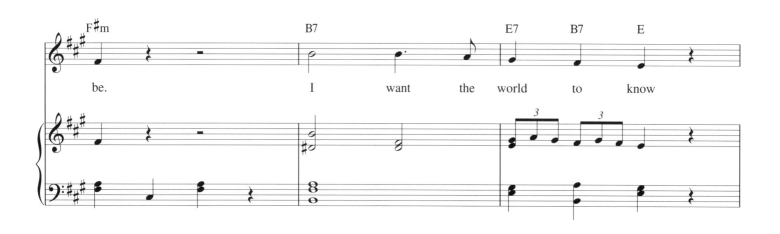

be. I want the world to know

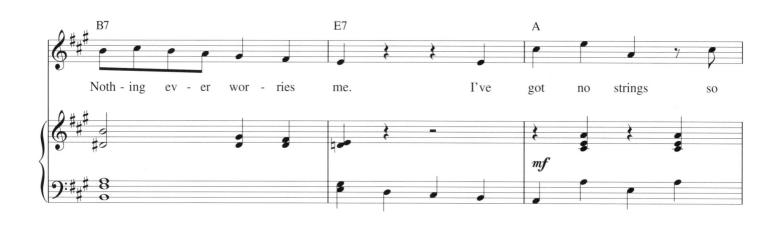

Noth - ing ev - er wor - ries me. I've got no strings so

I have fun, I'm not tied up to an - y - one,

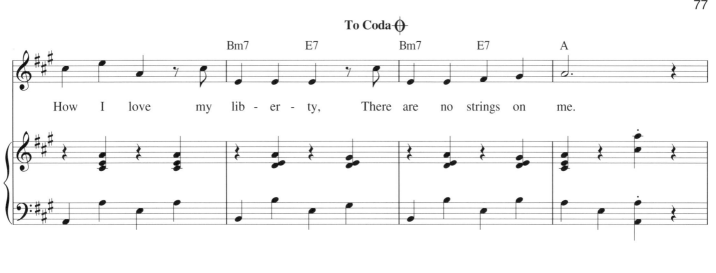

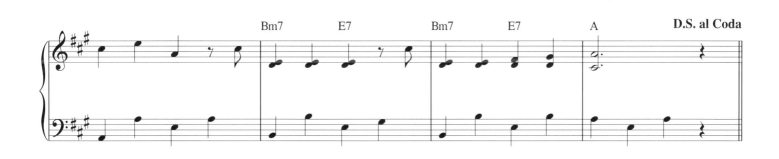

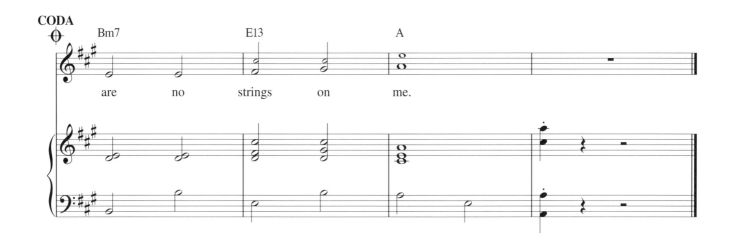

I'M LATE
from Walt Disney's *Alice in Wonderland*

Words by Bob Hilliard
Music by Sammy Fain

I'M WISHING
from Walt Disney's *Snow White and the Seven Dwarfs*

Words by Larry Morey
Music by Frank Churchill

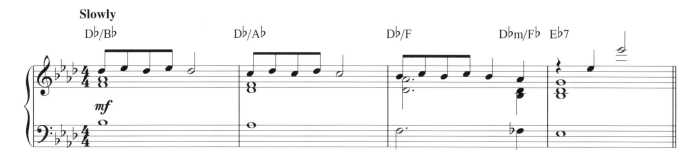

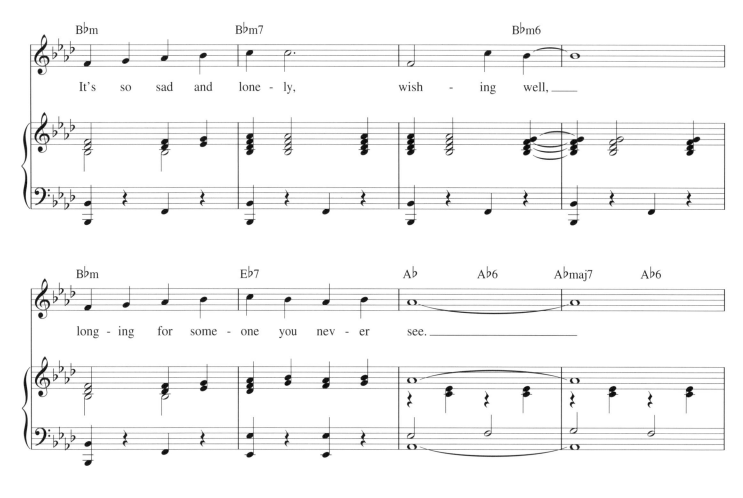

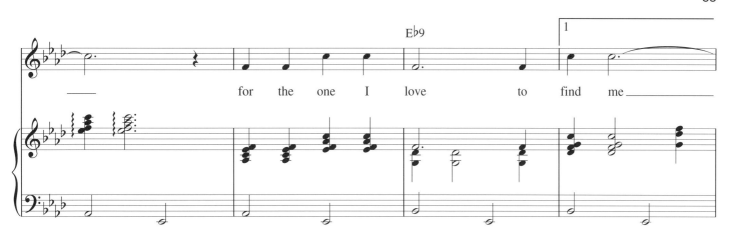

for the one I love to find me

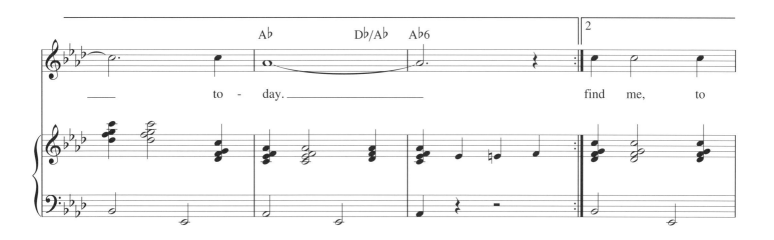

to - day. find me, to

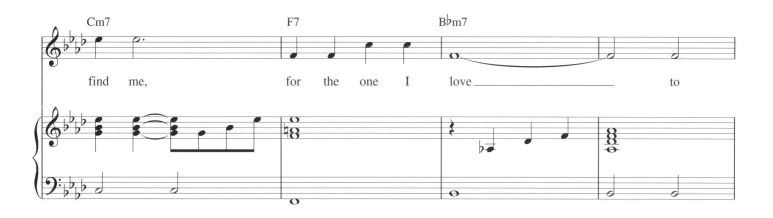

find me, for the one I love to

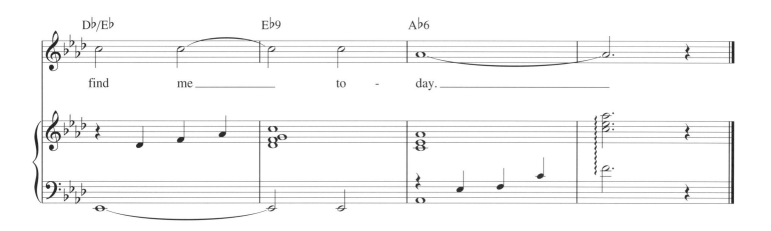

find me to - day.

IF I NEVER KNEW YOU

(Love Theme from *Pocahontas*)
from Walt Disney's *Pocahontas*

Music by Alan Menken
Lyrics by Stephen Schwartz

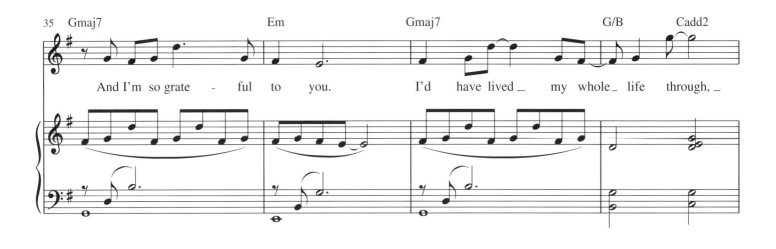

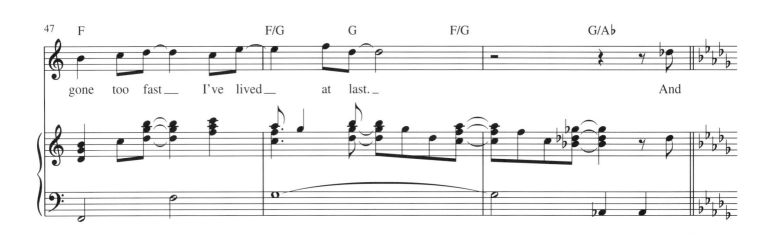

JUST AROUND THE RIVERBEND
from Walt Disney's *Pocahontas*

Music by Alan Menken
Lyrics by Stephen Schwartz

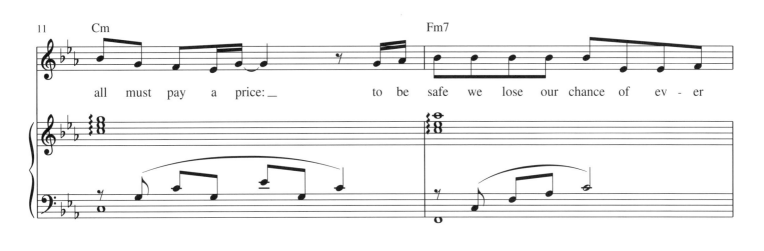

11 Cm / Fm7

all must pay a price:_ to be safe we lose our chance of ev - er

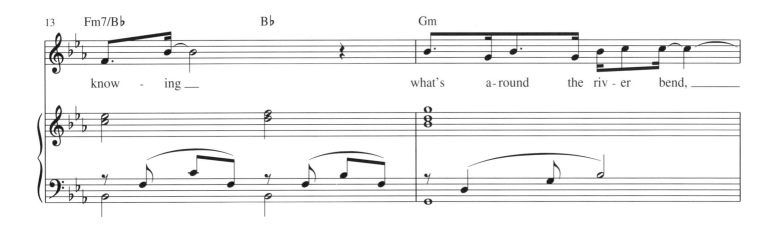

13 Fm7/B♭ / B♭ / Gm

know - ing _ what's a-round the riv - er bend, ___

15 A♭ / A♭/B♭ / Gm/B♭

_ wait - ing just a-round the riv - er bend. __

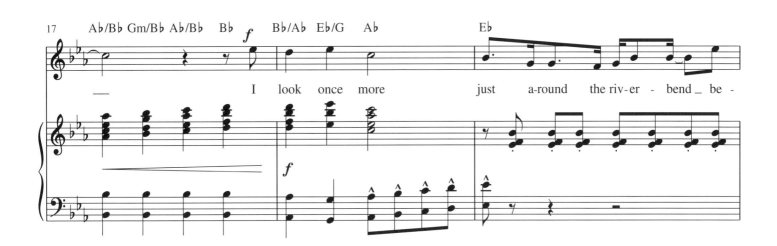

17 A♭/B♭ Gm/B♭ A♭/B♭ B♭ **f** B♭/A♭ E♭/G A♭ / E♭

I look once more just a-round the riv - er - bend _ be -

LAVENDER BLUE
(Dilly Dilly)
from Walt Disney's *So Dear to My Heart*

Words by Larry Morey
Music by Eliot Daniel

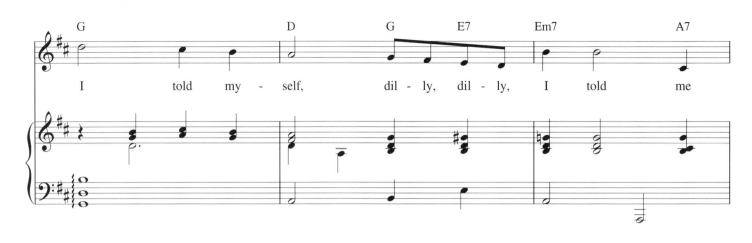

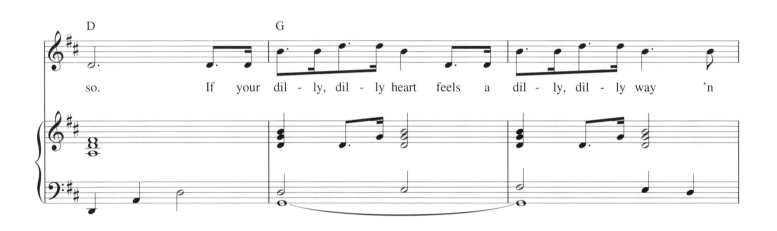

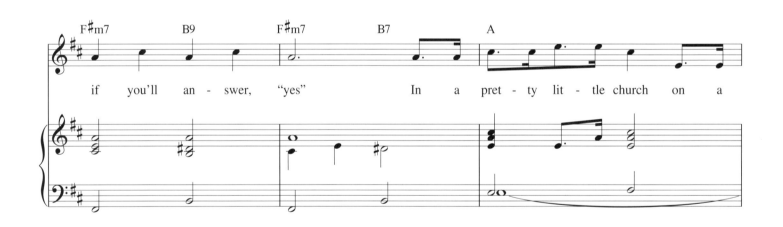

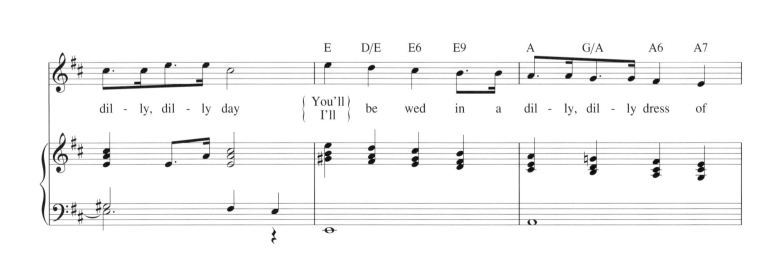

LES POISSONS
from Walt Disney's *The Little Mermaid*

Lyrics by Howard Ashman
Music by Alan Menken

100

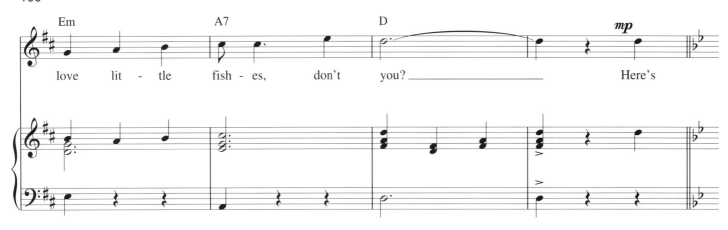

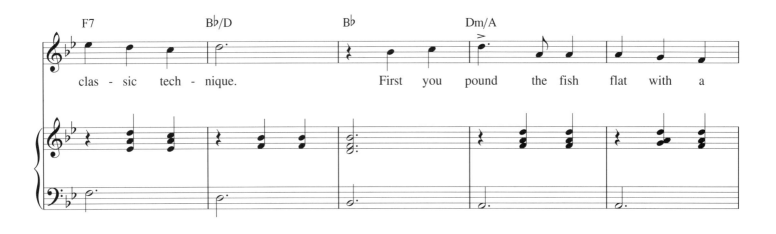

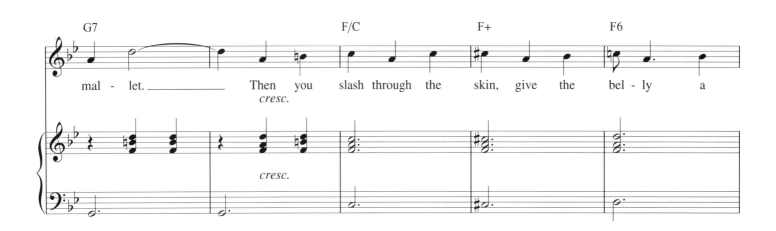

REFLECTION
from Walt Disney Pictures' *Mulan*

Music by Matthew Wilder
Lyrics by David Zippel

be my-self, I would break my fam - 'ly's ___ heart. ___

Who is that girl I ___ see

star - ing straight back at me? Why is my re - flec - tion some - one

I don't know? ___ Some - how I

THE LORD IS GOOD TO ME

from Walt Disney's *Melody Time*
from Walt Disney's *Johnny Appleseed*

Words and Music by Kim Gannon
and Walter Kent

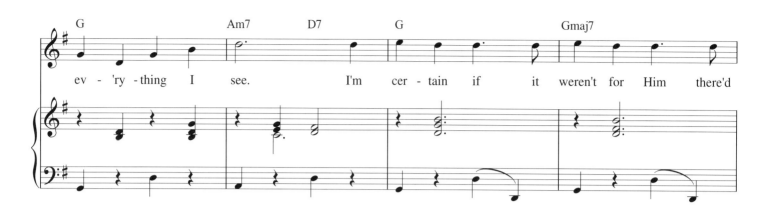

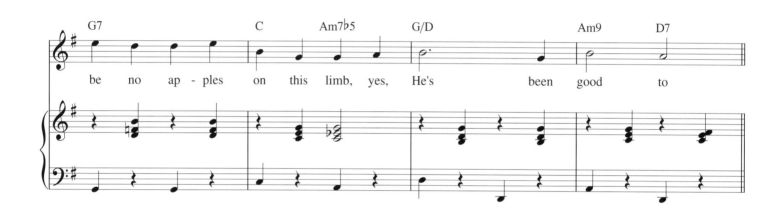

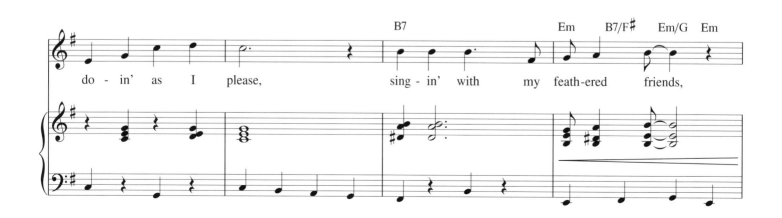

LOVE IS A SONG
from Walt Disney's *Bambi*

Words by Larry Morey
Music by Frank Churchill

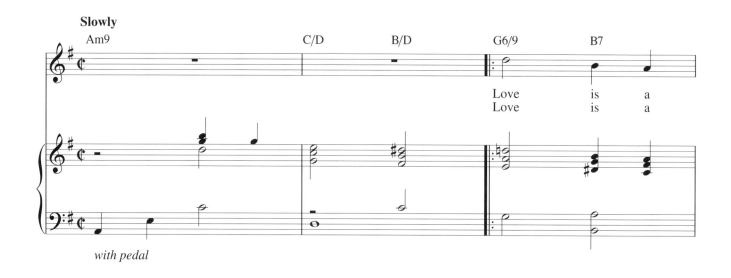

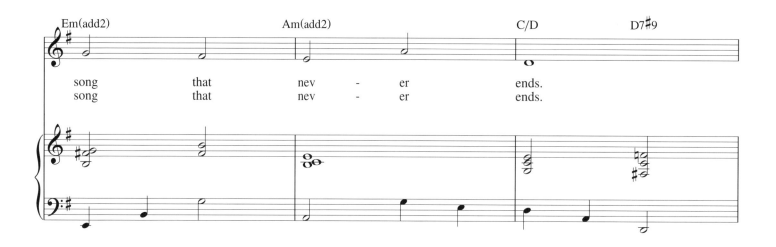

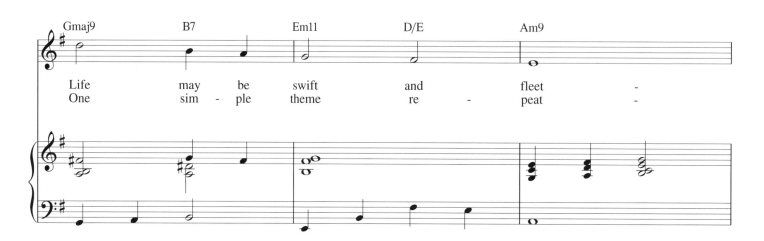

ONCE UPON A DREAM
from Walt Disney's *Sleeping Beauty*

Words and Music by Sammy Fain
and Jack Lawrence
Adapted from a Theme by Tchaikovsky

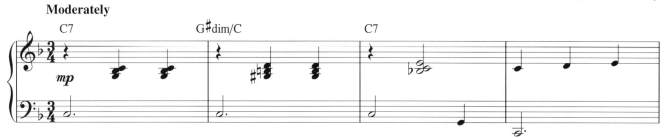

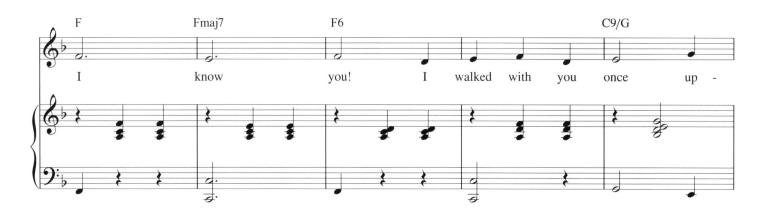

PART OF YOUR WORLD

from Walt Disney's *The Little Mermaid*

Lyrics by Howard Ashman
Music by Alan Menken

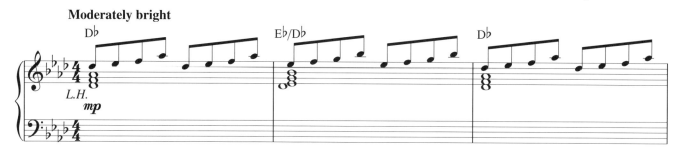

Moderately bright

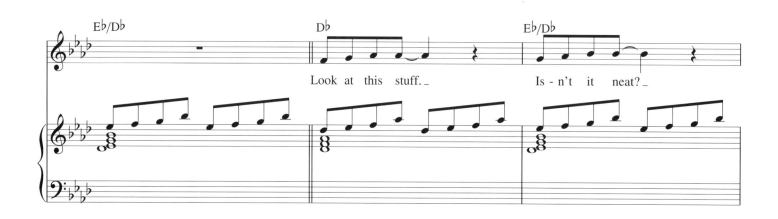

Look at this stuff. _ Is - n't it neat? _

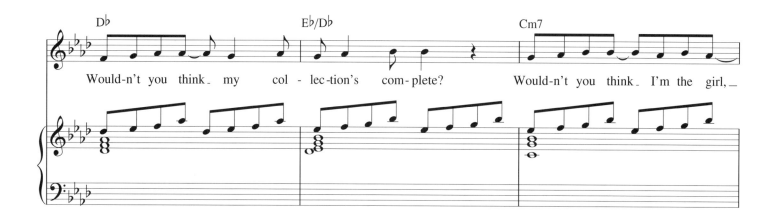

Would-n't you think _ my col - lec-tion's com - plete? Would-n't you think _ I'm the girl, _

_ the girl who has ev - 'ry - thing. _

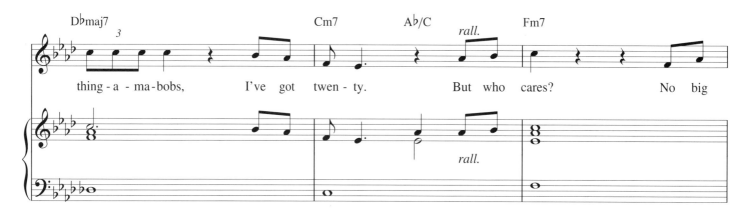

thing-a-ma-bobs, I've got twen-ty. But who cares? No big

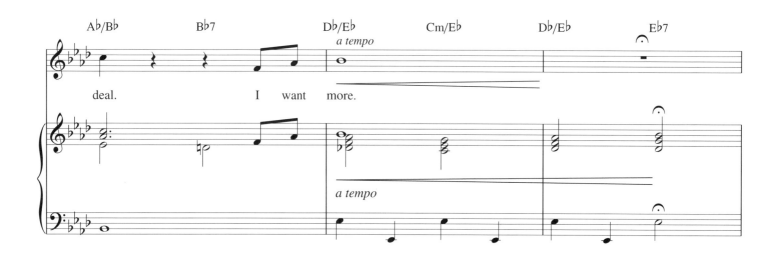

deal. I want more.

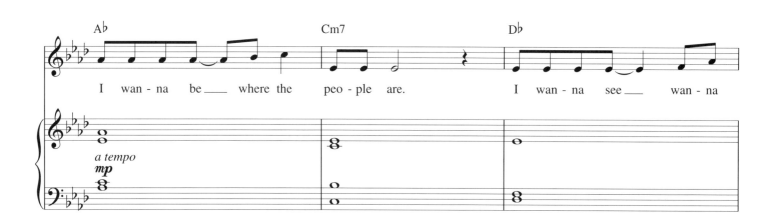

I wan-na be___ where the peo-ple are. I wan-na see___ wan-na

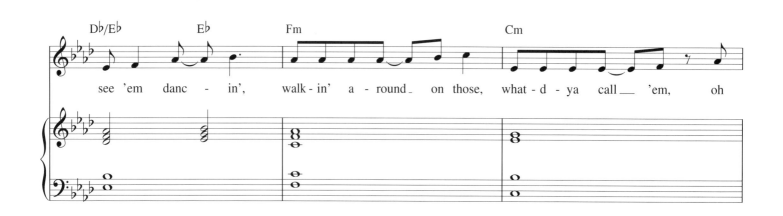

see 'em danc-in', walk-in' a-round___ on those, what-d-ya call___ 'em, oh

118

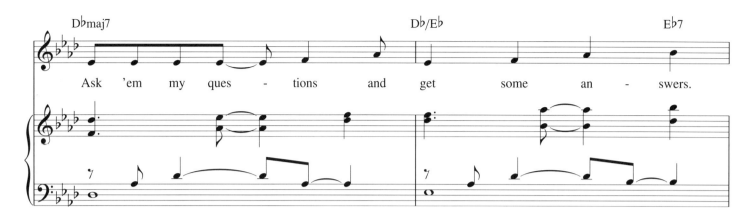

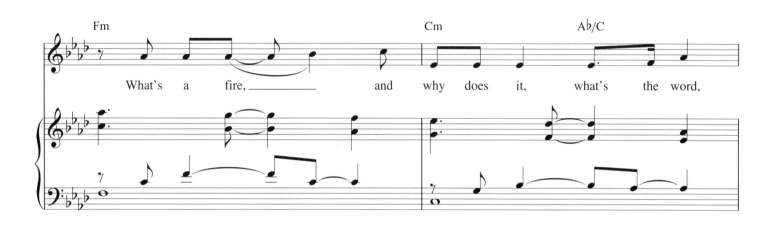

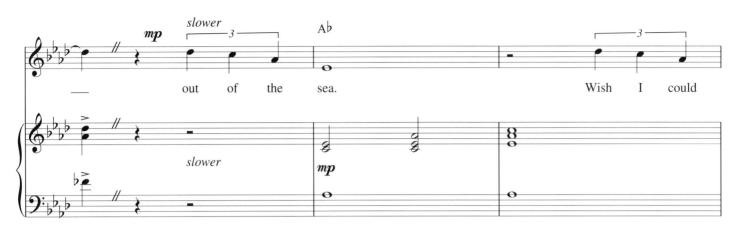

out of the sea. Wish I could

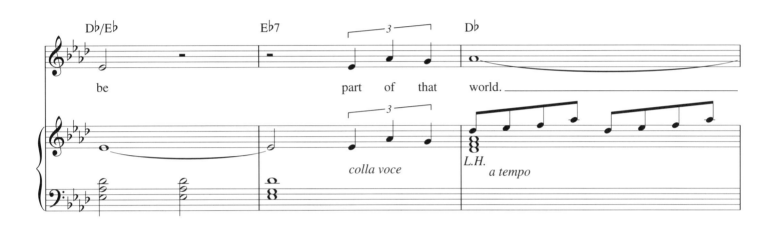

be part of that world.

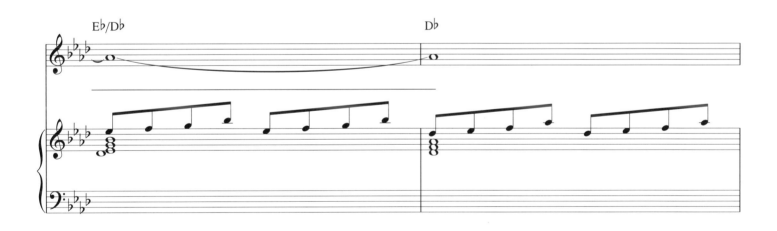

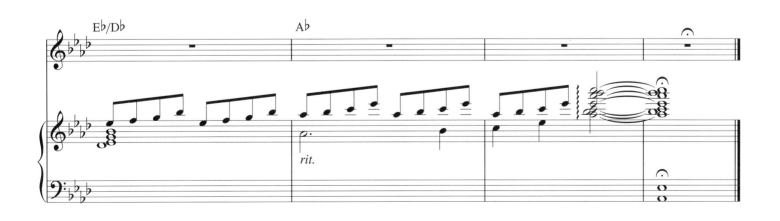

SANTA FE
from Walt Disney's *Newsies*

Lyrics by Jack Feldman
Music by Alan Menken

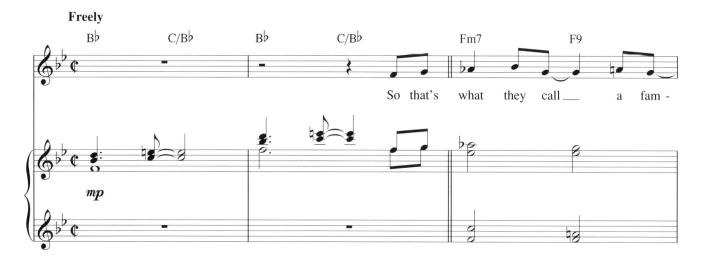

So that's what they call ___ a fam-

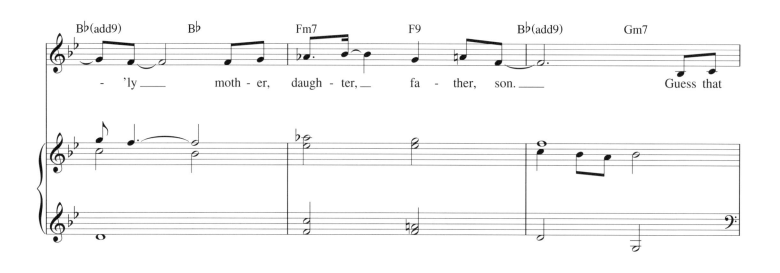

-'ly ___ moth-er, daugh-ter, ___ fa-ther, son. ___ Guess that

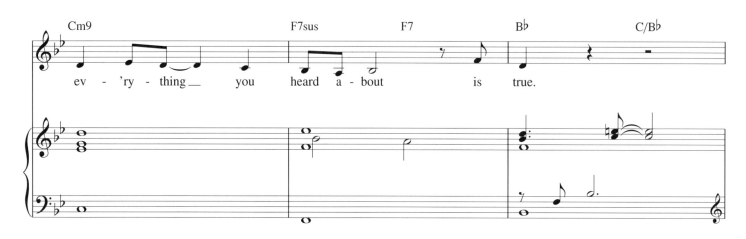

ev-'ry-thing ___ you heard a-bout is true.

So you ain't got an-y fam - 'ly. ___ Well, who said you need-ed one? Ain't ya glad no-bod-y's wait-in' up for you? When I dream on my own I'm a-lone but I ain't

lone - ly.   For   a   dream - er,   night's   the   on - ly   time   of   day. __

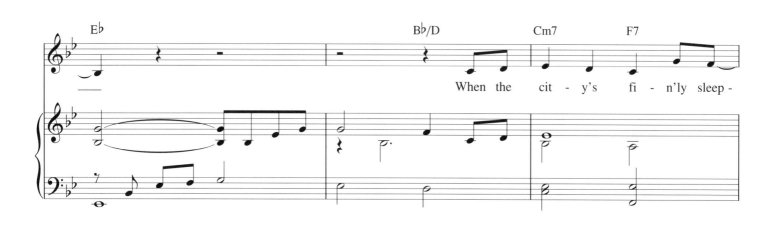

__   When   the   cit - y's   fi - n'ly   sleep -

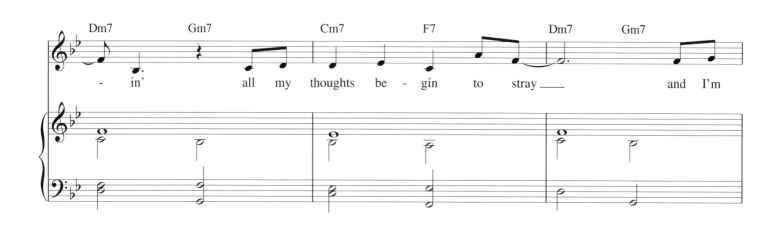

- in'   all   my   thoughts   be - gin   to   stray __   and   I'm

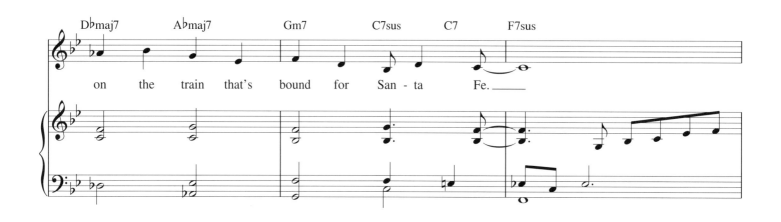

on   the   train   that's   bound   for   San - ta   Fe. __

Dreams come true. Yes, they do _____ in San - ta Fe. _____

Somewhat faster

Where does it say you got - ta live and die here?

Where does it say a guy can't catch a break?

Why should you on - ly take what you're giv - en? Why should you spend your

128

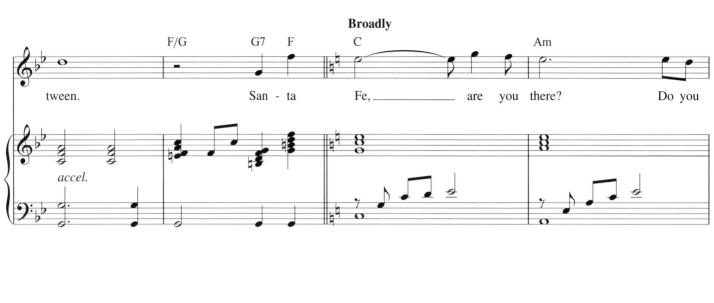

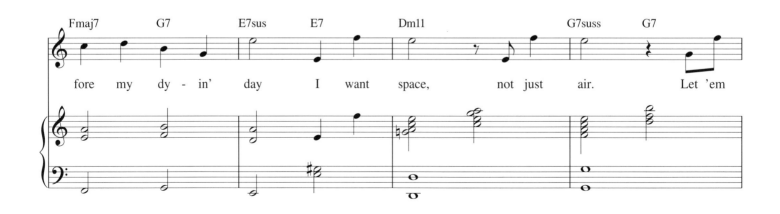

THE SECOND STAR TO THE RIGHT

from Walt Disney's *Peter Pan*

Words by Sammy Cahn
Music by Sammy Fain

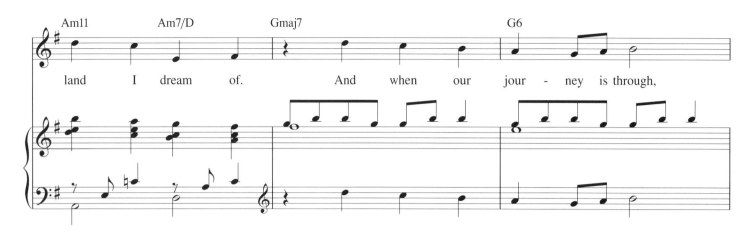

land I dream of. And when our jour - ney is through,

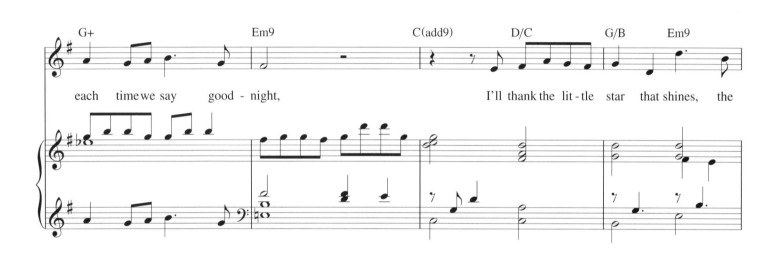

each time we say good - night, I'll thank the lit - tle star that shines, the

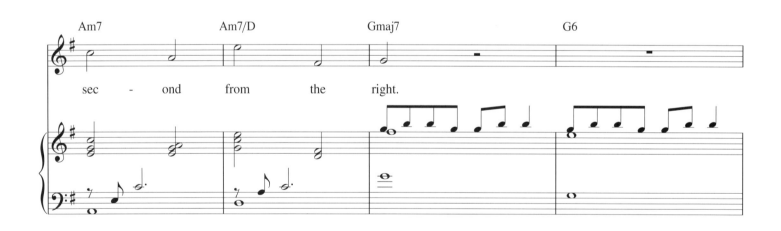

sec - ond from the right.

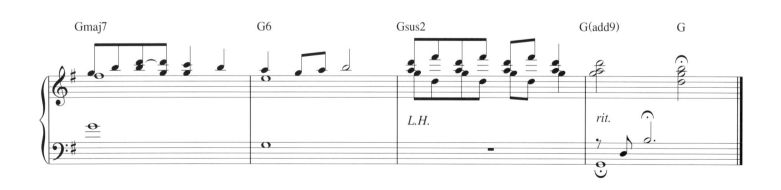

SING A SMILING SONG
from Walt Disney's *Sleeping Beauty*

Words by Tom Adair
Music by George Bruns
Adapted from a Theme by Tchaikovsky

SO THIS IS LOVE
(The Cinderella Waltz)
from Walt Disney's *Cinderella*

Words and Music by Mack David,
Al Hoffman and Jerry Livingston

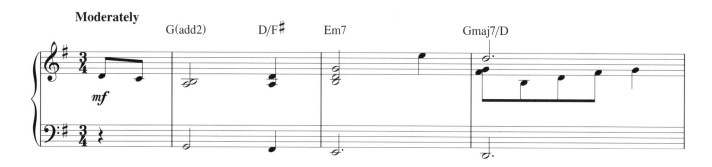

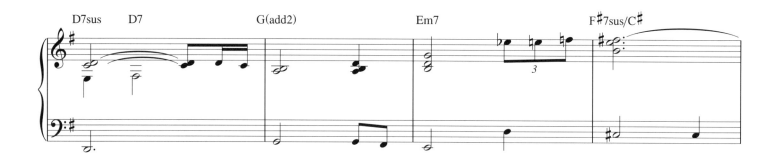

So this is love. ____ You can search

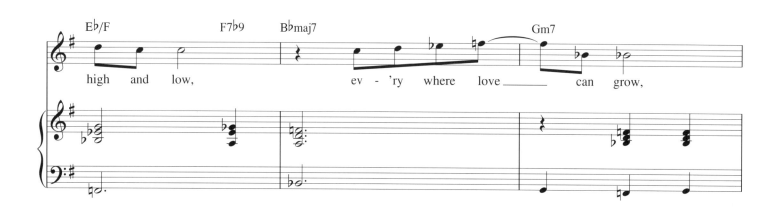

high and low, ev - 'ry where love _____ can grow,

then one day it's here with the wind.

On - ly a dream a - way, wait - ing for you

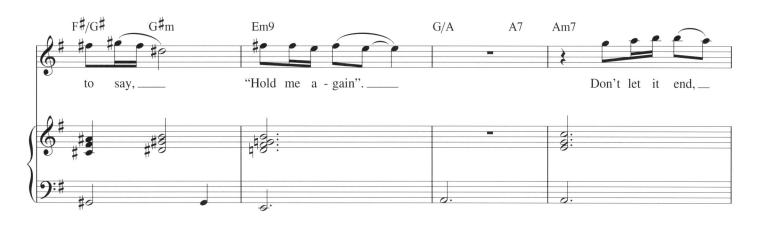

to say, _____ "Hold me a - gain". _____ Don't let it end, __

don't _____ let it end, please, ba - by. __

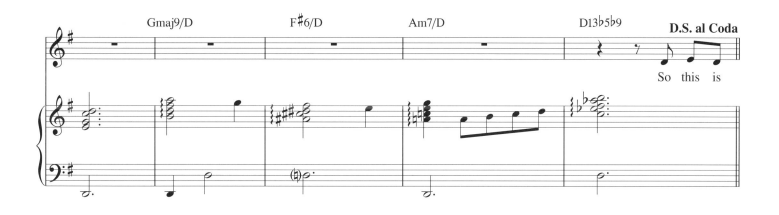

So this is

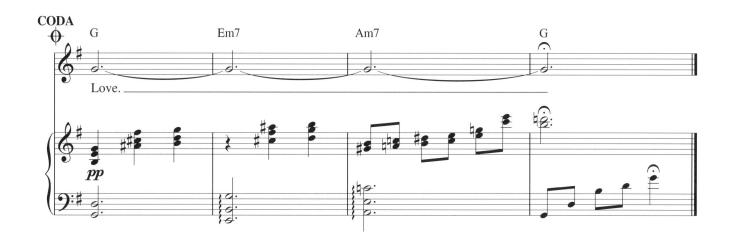

Love. _____

SOME DAY MY PRINCE WILL COME

from Walt Disney's *Snow White and the Seven Dwarfs*

Words by Larry Morey
Music by Frank Churchill

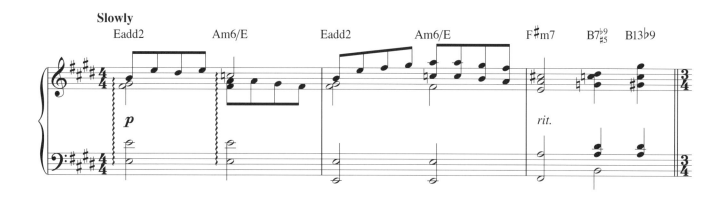

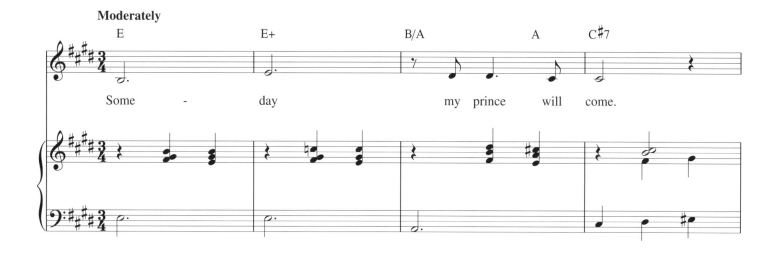

far a - way, I'll find my love some - day, some -

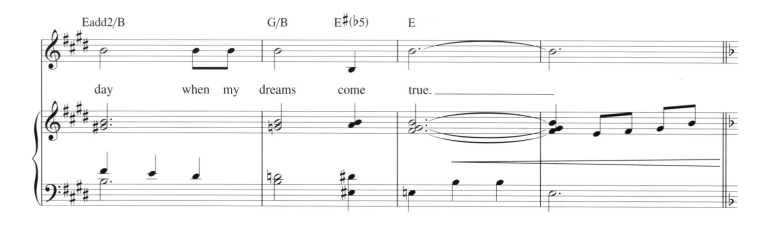

day when my dreams come true._____

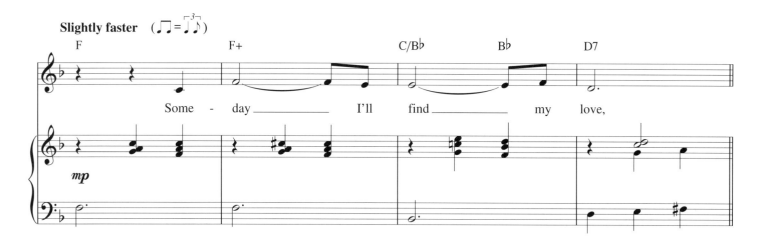

Some - day_____ I'll find_____ my love,

some - one_____ to call_____ my own. And I'll

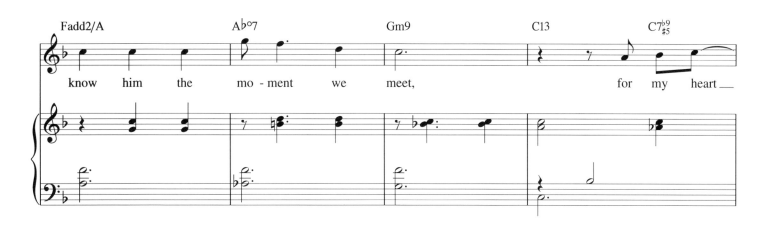

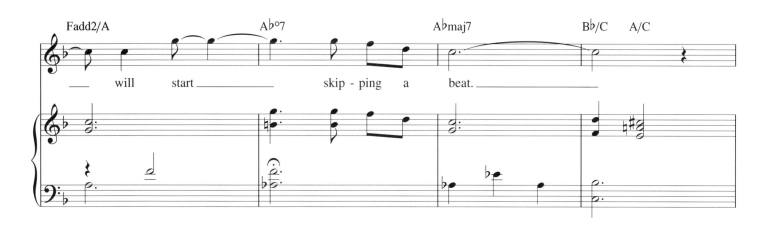

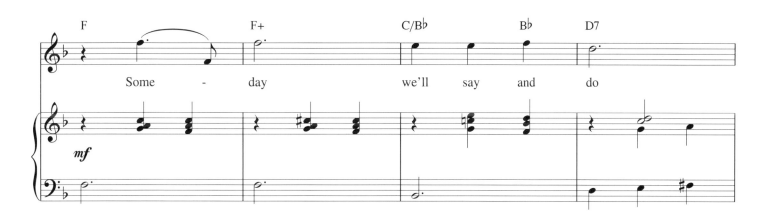

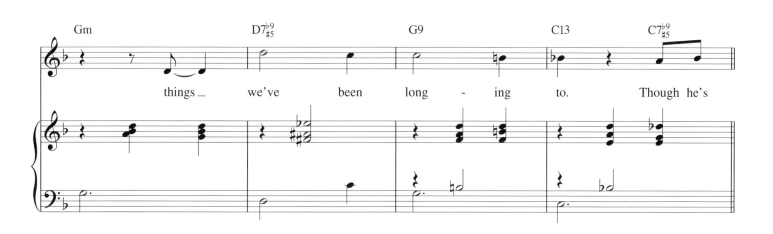

146

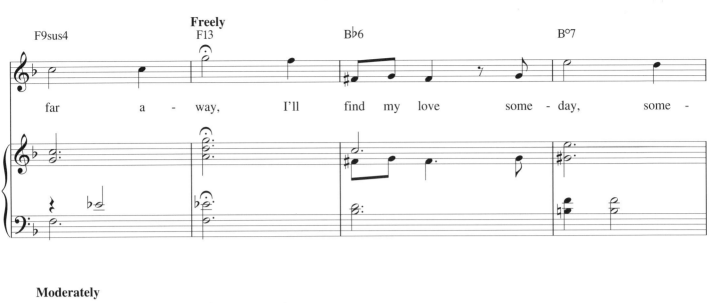

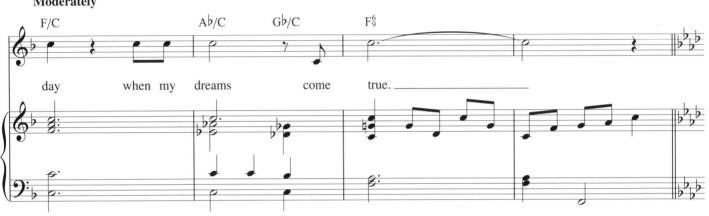

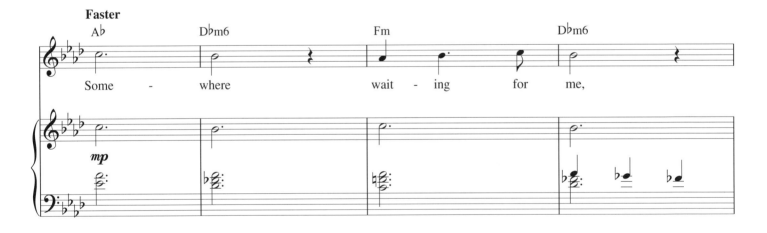

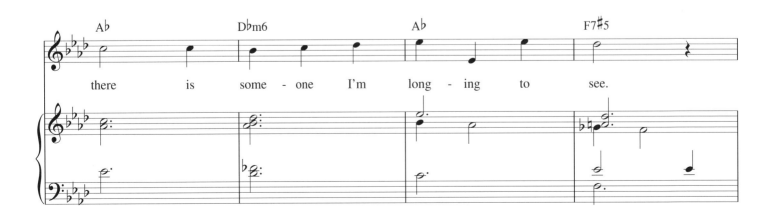

far a - way, I'll find my love some - day,

Slightly slower

some - day when my dreams come true. _____

Freely

Oh, please make my dreams come

true. _____

WHEN I SEE AN ELEPHANT FLY

from Walt Disney's *Dumbo*

Words by Ned Washington
Music by Oliver Wallace

SOMEDAY

from Walt Disney's *The Hunchback of Notre Dame*

Music by Alan Menken
Lyrics by Stephen Schwartz

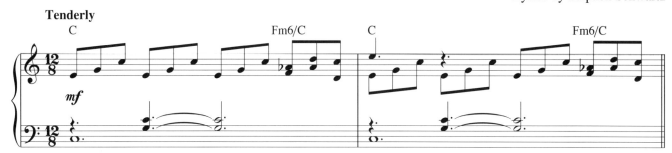

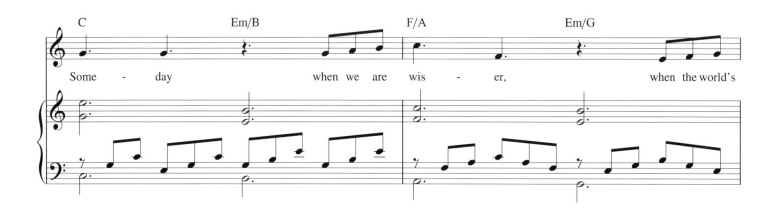

Some - day when we are wis - er, when the world's

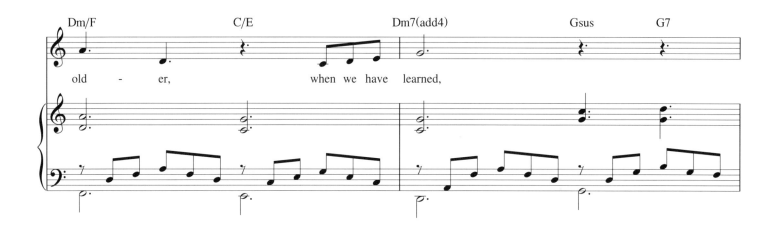

old - er, when we have learned,

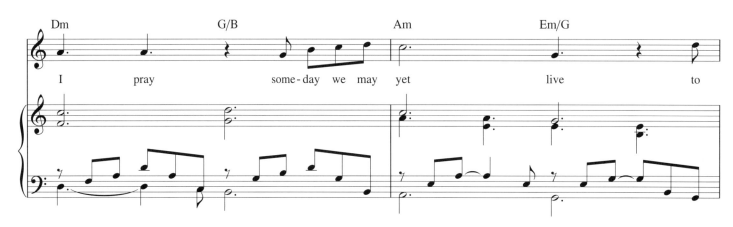

I pray some - day we may yet live to

on its way. Let it come some - day.

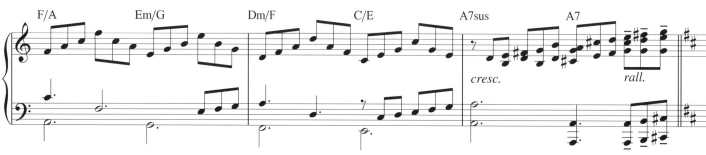

Broadly

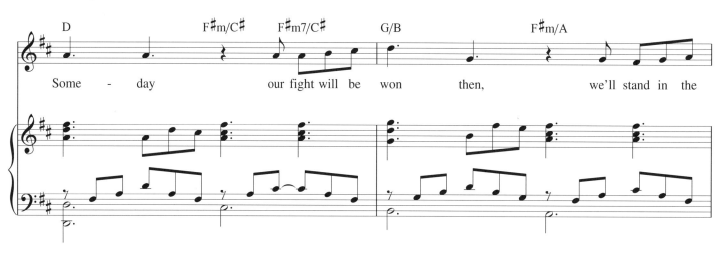

Some - day our fight will be won then, we'll stand in the

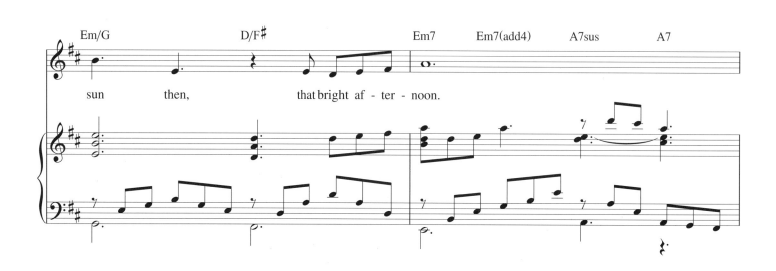

sun then, that bright af - ter - noon.

SOONER OR LATER

from Walt Disney's *Song of the South*

Words and Music by Ray Gilbert
and Charles Wolcott

A SPOONFUL OF SUGAR

from Walt Disney's *Mary Poppins*

Words and Music by Richard M. Sherman
and Robert B. Sherman

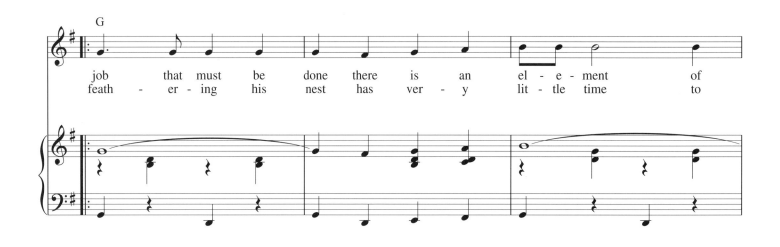

job that must be done there is an el - e - ment of
feath - er - ing his nest has ver - y lit - tle time to

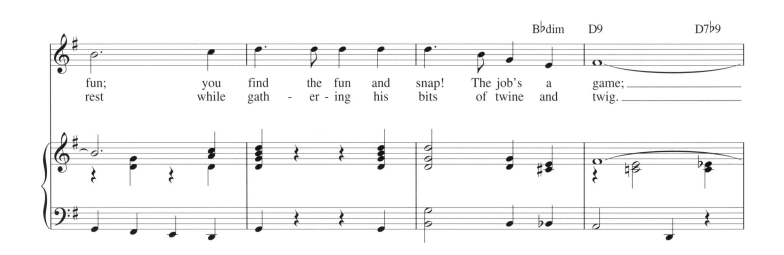

fun; you find the fun and snap! The job's a game; ___
rest while gath - er - ing his bits of twine and twig. ___

WHEN SHE LOVED ME
from Walt Disney Pictures' *Toy Story 2* - A Pixar Film

Music and Lyrics by
Randy Newman

WHEN YOU WISH UPON A STAR

from Walt Disney's *Pinocchio*

Words by Ned Washington
Music by Leigh Harline

A WHOLE NEW WORLD
from Walt Disney's *Aladdin*

Music by Alan Menken
Lyrics by Tim Rice

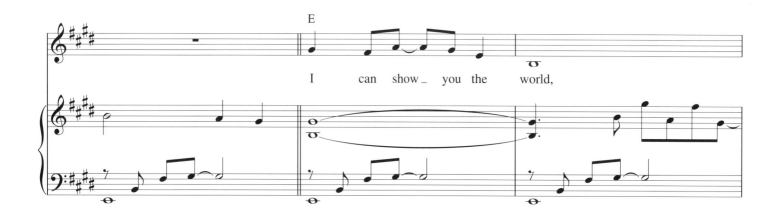

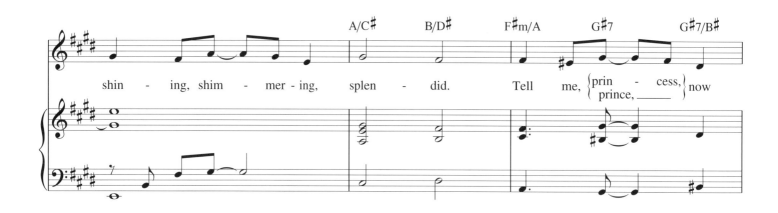

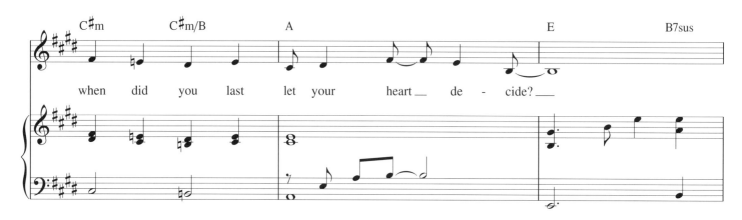

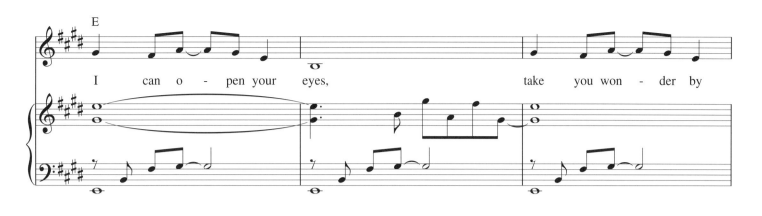

I can o - pen your eyes, take you won - der by

won - der, o - ver, side - ways and un - der on a

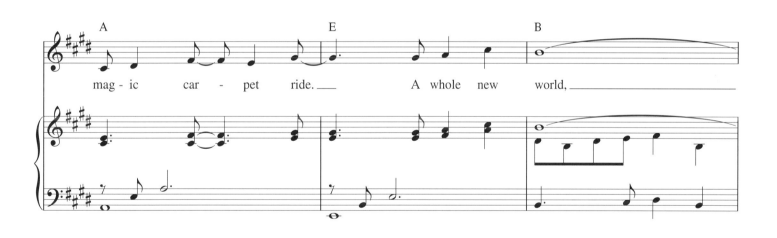

mag - ic car - pet ride. ___ A whole new world, _____

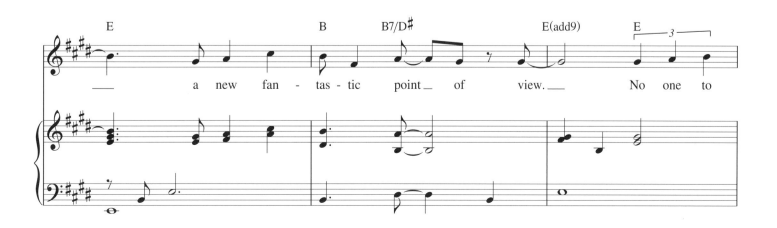

___ a new fan - tas - tic point ___ of view. ___ No one to

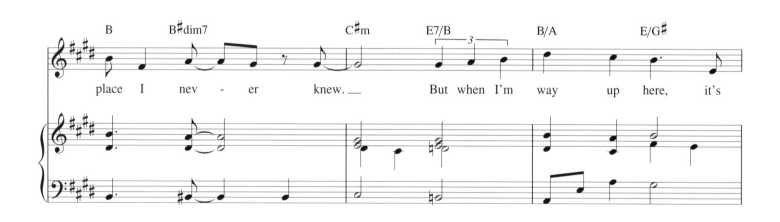

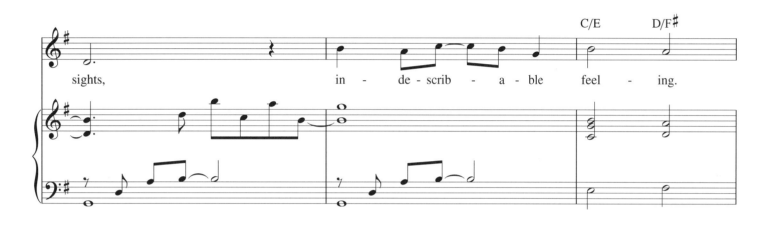

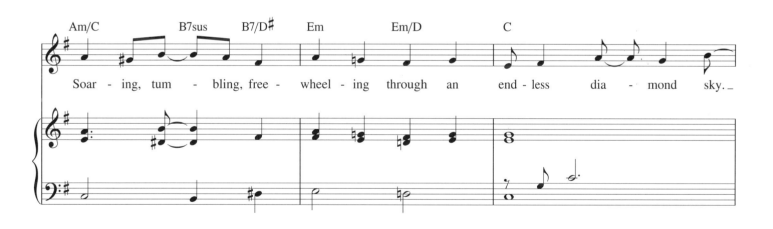

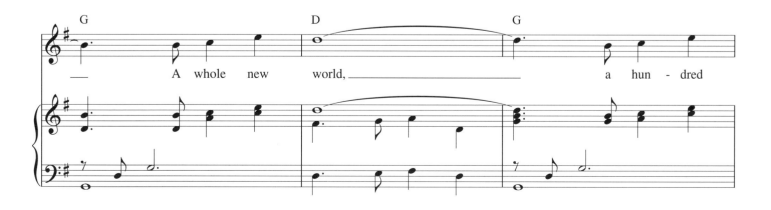

thou - sand things be - gin. I'm like a shoot - ing star, I've

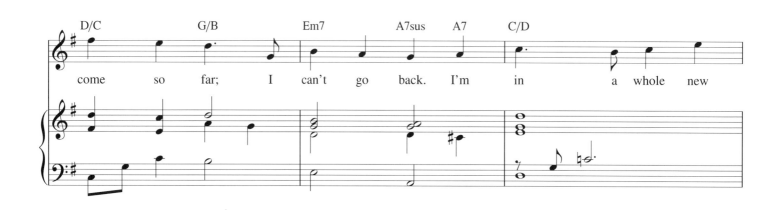

come so far; I can't go back. I'm in a whole new

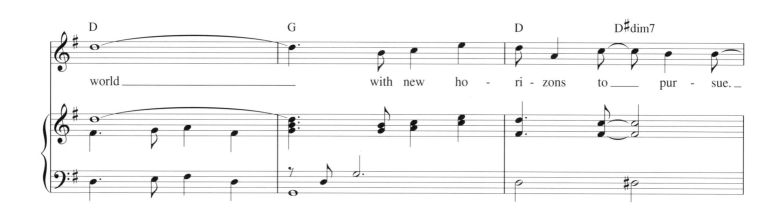

world _____ with new ho - ri - zons to ____ pur - sue. __

__ I'll chase them an - y - where. There's time to spare.

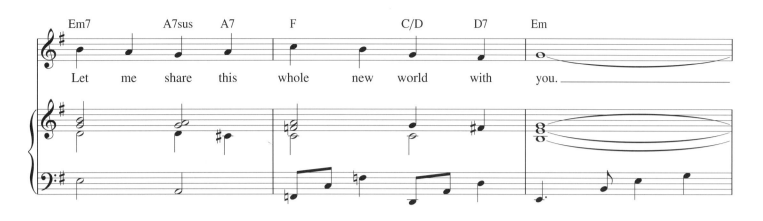

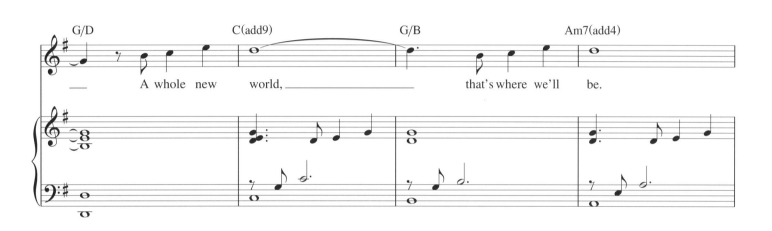

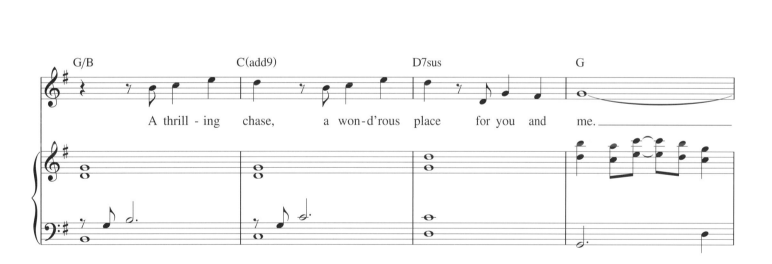

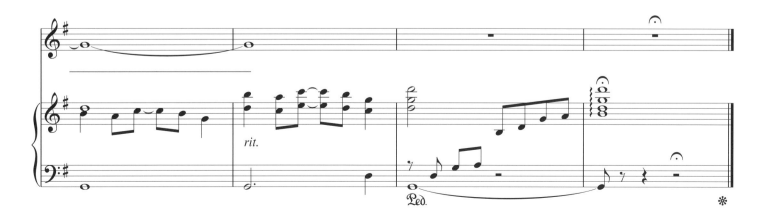

WITH A SMILE AND A SONG
from Walt Disney's *Snow White and the Seven Dwarfs*

Words by Larry Morey
Music by Frank Churchill

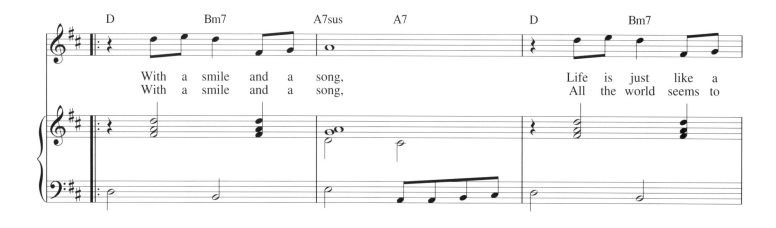

With a smile and a song,
With a smile and a song,

Life is just like a
All the world seems to

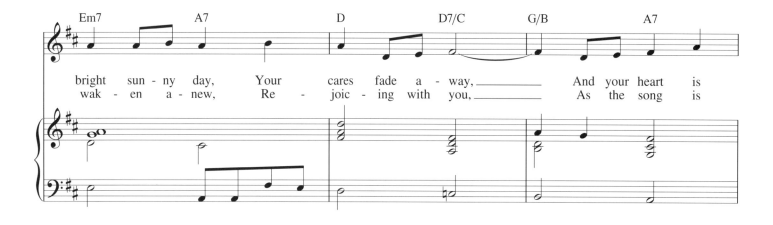

bright sun-ny day, Your cares fade a-way,_____ And your heart is
wak-en a-new, Re-joic-ing with you,_____ As the song is

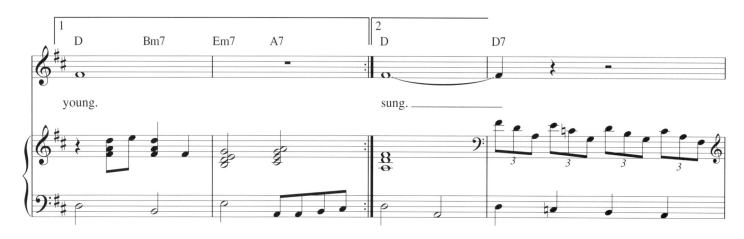

young.

sung._____

THE WORK SONG
from Walt Disney's *Cinderella*

Words and Music by Mack David
Al Hoffman and Jerry Livingston

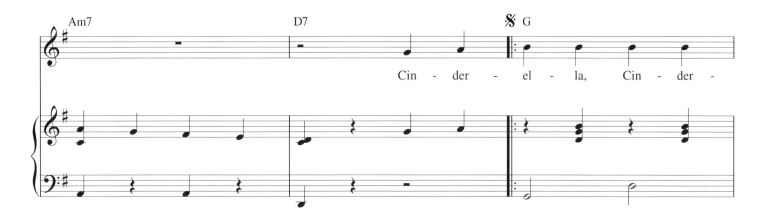

Cin - der - el - la, Cin - der -

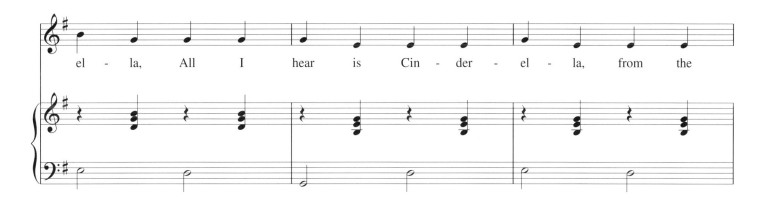

el - la, All I hear is Cin - der - el - la, from the

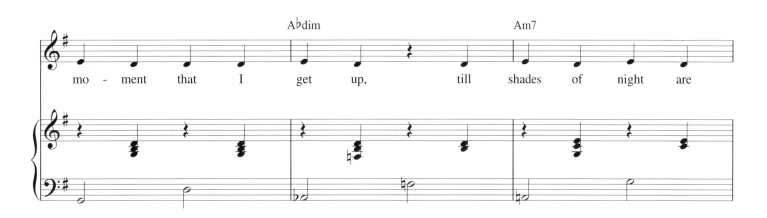

mo - ment that I get up, till shades of night are

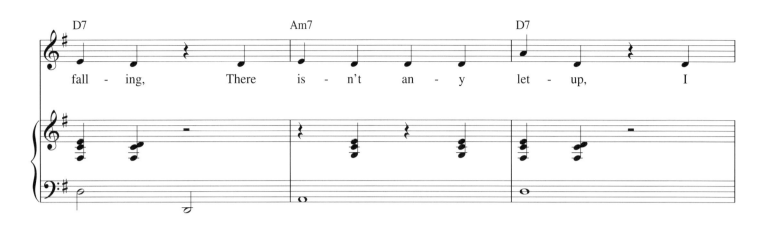

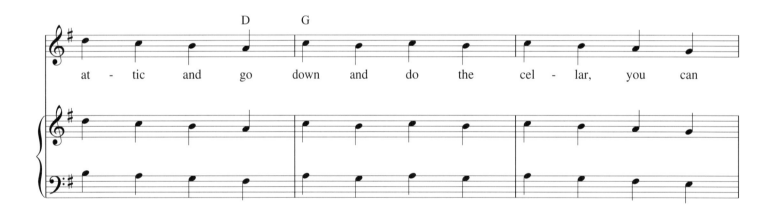

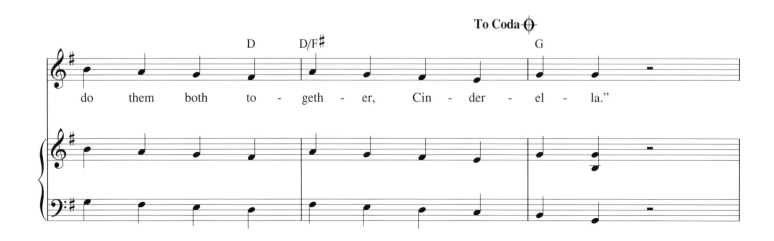

YOU'VE GOT A FRIEND IN ME

from Walt Disney's *Toy Story*

Music and Lyrics by
Randy Newman

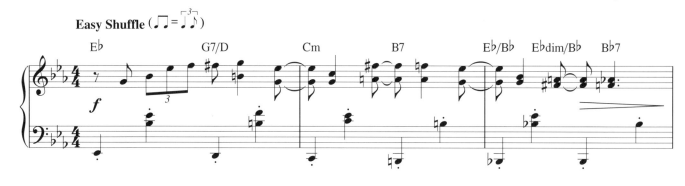

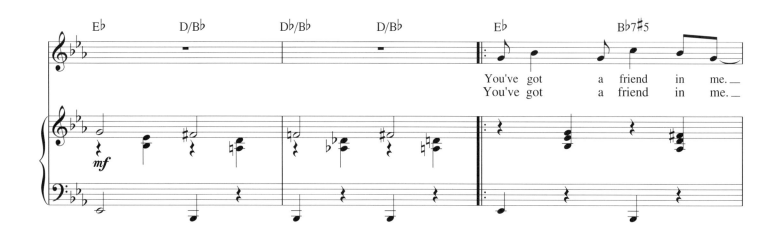

You've got a friend in me.
You've got a friend in me.

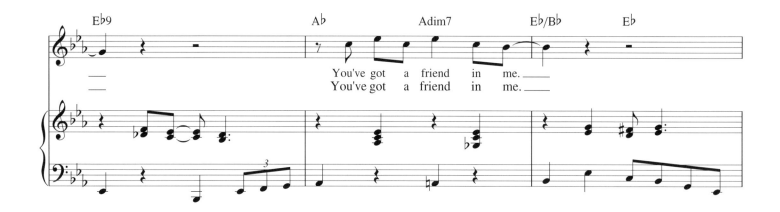

You've got a friend in me.
You've got a friend in me.

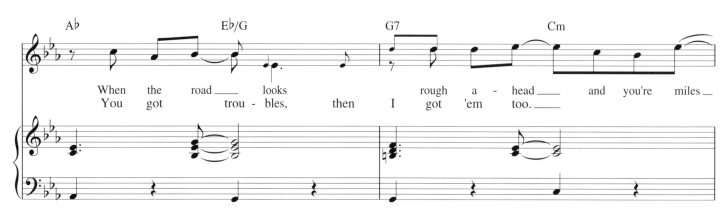

When the road looks rough a-head and you're miles
You got trou-bles, then I got 'em too.

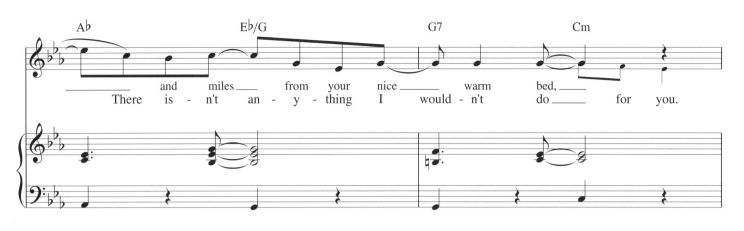

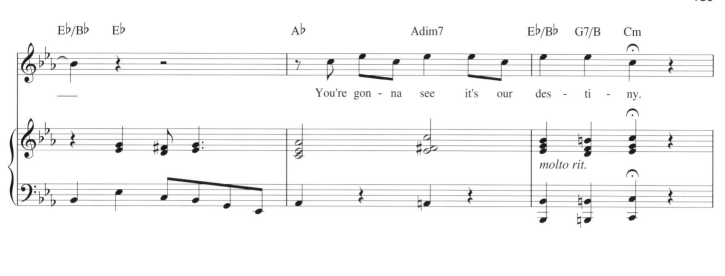

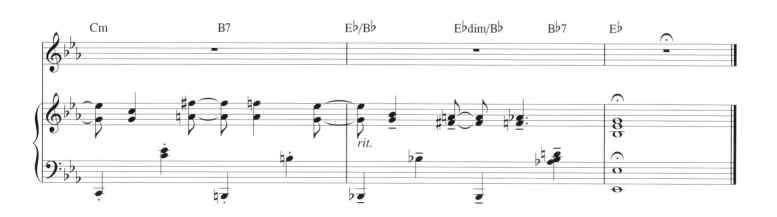

ZIP-A-DEE-DOO-DAH
from Walt Disney's *Song of the South*

Words by Ray Gilbert
Music by Allie Wrubel